WITHDRAWN

The Speechwriter

A Brief Education in Politics

Barton Swaim

SIMON & SCHUSTER

New York London Toronto Sydney New Delhi

Simon & Schuster
1230 Avenue of the Americas
New York, NY 10020

First Simon & Schuster hardcover edition July 2015

SIMON & SCHUSTER and colophon are registered trademarks
of Simon & Schuster, Inc.

For information about special discounts for bulk purchases,
please contact Simon & Schuster Special Sales at 1-866-506-1949
or business@simonandschuster.com.

The Simon & Schuster Speakers Bureau can bring authors to your
live event. For more information or to book an event contact the
Simon & Schuster Speakers Bureau at 1-866-248-3049 or visit our
website at www.simonspeakers.com.

Interior design by Lewelin Polanco

Manufactured in the United States of America

10 9 8 7 6 5 4 3 2 1

Library of Congress Cataloging-in-Publication Data

Swaim, Barton, 1972–
   The speechwriter : a brief education in politics / Barton Swaim. — First
Simon & Schuster hardcover edition.
      pages cm
   1. Sanford, Mark, 1960– 2. Sanford, Mark, 1960– —Friends and associates.
3. South Carolina—Politics and government—1951– 4. Swaim, Barton, 1972–
5. Speechwriters—South Carolina—Biography. I. Title.
F275.42.S26S94 2015
328.3'3092—dc23
[B]
                                                             2014047506

ISBN 978-1-4767-6992-9
ISBN 978-1-4767-6996-7 (ebook)

In the multitude of words there wanteth not sin.

—Book of Proverbs

CONTENTS

Contents

viii

Contents

AUTHOR'S NOTE

This memoir is based on the three years and ten months I spent working for the governor of a southern state. I have taken some liberties with chronology, many of the names are changed, as are some identifying and other details, and some of the dialogue is imperfectly remembered I'm sure.

I didn't write the book to pay anybody back or to reveal lurid secrets and inside scoops. I wrote it because I had to. I am a writer, and a writer can't witness the kinds of things I did without writing them down for someone else to enjoy.

A few passages appeared originally as essays in the *Times Literary Supplement*'s "Freelance" column, and I am grateful to James Campbell for accepting them and urging me to make them better. I'm also grateful to my editor at Simon & Schuster, Priscilla Painton, who made this book far better than it was.

The Speechwriter

1

THE DUMPS

About twenty of us sat in the conference room waiting for the boss to walk in. The room was warm and smelled faintly of sweat. A pair of law clerks quietly debated the correct pronunciation of "debacle." At last Paul asked what the meeting was about. "I think," June said, "the governor wants to apologize to the staff." She said it with a wry look, but nobody laughed.

Stewart looked up from a magazine. "He already did that," he snapped. "He apologized to his mistress, and to his family—."

"In that order," Paul said.

Nervous laughter made its way around the room.

"I don't think we can handle another apology," Stewart

went on, throwing down the magazine. "Because let me tell you, I know what an apology from this governor sounds like, and it ain't really an apology. It's more like—."

He paused.

Someone said, "More like what?"

"I'll just put it this way. His apologies tend to have an un-apologetic tone."

Another minute passed, and then the governor walked in. All went silent. He sat in the only remaining chair and made jokes with one of the interns.

A week before, he had been openly talked about by influential commentators in New York and Washington as a presidential candidate. In national media reports, his name had been routinely used in conjunction with the terms "principled stand," "courageous," "crazy," "unbalanced," and "interesting." The party's biggest donors had begun to call him and to pay him visits. Now he was the punch line to a thousand jokes; letters demanding his resignation appeared in newspapers; the word "impeachment" circulated through the capital like rumors of an assassination plot.

"How are y'all?" he said. "Wait—don't answer that."

More nervous laugher.

"Aahh." That was his preface to saying anything significant. "Aahh. But that's why I called you in here. I just wanted to say the obvious, which is the obvious."

Paul gave me a look of incomprehension.

"I mean, the obvious—which is that I caused the storm we're now in. And that's made everything a little more difficult for everybody in here, and for that I want to say the obvious, which is that I apologize. But you know"—he rose up in his seat to an upright posture—"you know, I was telling one of the boys"—the governor had four sons—"this morning. We were up early and I was saying, 'Look, the sun came up today.' It's a beautiful thing to see. And it's a beautiful thing regardless of the storms of life. Of which this is one."

People shifted in their seats and glanced at each other questioningly.

"As it happens," the governor went on, "and before this storm started, I'd been reading Viktor Frankl's book about being in a concentration camp. And it's just incredible to me how you can find beauty, you can find reasons to keep going, in the most appalling circumstances. And I just wanted to say to everybody, keep your head up. Keep pushing forward. And let's not be in the dumps here. The sun came up today. Aahh. We're not in a concentration camp. So let's not stay in the dumps. We can't make much progress on the important things if we're in the dumps. So if you're in the dumps, get out. I mean, of the dumps. Get out of the dumps."

Nobody spoke.

"Aahh. So, anybody want to say anything? Comments? Pearls of wisdom?"

Still no one spoke.

"Okay, well—."

"Actually I'd like to say something." That was Stella.

"Okay."

"I just want to say—. Actually maybe I shouldn't."

"No, it's okay," the governor smiled, "go ahead."

"No, I think I won't."

"You sure?"

"Mm. Yeah."

The governor walked out. Stewart looked around the room and said, "For those of you who are newer to the office, that was the governor's version of a pep talk. Do you feel pepped?"

Later that afternoon I asked Stella what she'd been intending to say. She had often told me that she didn't like her job—her husband wanted her to keep it for the income—and had often tried to get herself fired. I thought this might have been one of those times. She narrowed her eyes and pointed at me. "You know what I was about to say? You really want to know? I was going to say, 'You know what, governor—maybe what you say is true. Maybe we should be thankful that we're not in a concentration camp.'" You could hear a slight tremor in her voice. "'And maybe we take the sun rising for granted, and we shouldn't. But you're not really the one who should tell us that right now. And if you do say anything, it should be more like Sorry I flushed all your work down the toilet, people. Sorry I made you all a joke. Sorry about your next job interview, the one where you're going to be brought in as a curiosity and then laughed at.'"

"Stella, I wish you had said that."

She had tears in her eyes.

2

I first met the governor almost three years earlier. We were in his office with Rick, his chief of staff. I introduced myself; he said, "A pleasure"; and we sat down. He wore blue jeans and a navy polo. There was a bleached streak across the front of the polo, which was untucked. His half-eaten lunch, a sandwich and chips, sat in Styrofoam on the coffee table in front of him. He took another bite of it, eating only the interior of the sandwich with a fork, and mumbled an apology for eating. Then he closed the Styrofoam box, pushed it aside, and sat upright.

For a few long seconds he said nothing. Then it seemed he wanted to speak. His mouth formed a circle, as if whatever he wanted to say began with a *w*.

"Wwwww," he said, staring upward. Then he fixed his eyes on Rick. "Wwwwwha."

Rick seemed ready to interject, but at last the governor said, "Www. What are we doing here?"

Rick introduced me. "He's here to talk about joining us in the press office. He's a writer."

"Oh, the writer." Now engaged, the governor looked at me and asked if I knew some name or other. I said I didn't. He said this guy had had the job before me, that he'd been a writer at *The State*. He was a good guy. But he'd had to tell him it wasn't working out and he needed to find something else. The governor hadn't kicked him out onto the streets, he said, just told him he needed to find something else. "He couldn't find my voice."

The governor was "very interested in this larger idea of a brand," he said. Every written product with his name on it had to be in the same style and have the same "cadence"; people should be able to read it and know it was his, whether or not they agreed with it. He mentioned the name of a famous politician and the name of his speechwriter. "Every speech he gives, every op-ed or whatever, sounds the same. Not the same, like boring the same. From the same source, consistent. I like that. It's about consistency. You always know what you're getting."

I said consistency was a good thing in a politician. It suggested reliability. I thought I'd blundered in using the word "politician," but he said, "Reliability. That's a good word for it."

He had seen some articles and reviews I'd written and

6

conceded I must be "erudite" but wondered whether I could write in a way that "the mechanic in Greenwood can understand." (Greenwood is a small town in the western part of the state.) I was trying to explain that I could when he interrupted me. "Can you start a sentence with a preposition?"

"A preposition?" I asked. Yes, a preposition. Maybe he meant a conjunction?

"Wwwhatever," he said.

"Well, it depends."

"On what?"

I said the rule against beginning sentences with conjunctions was a very old rule and nobody really followed it anymore. Also, initial conjunctions are useful. In a tightly reasoned paragraph you need to turn your argument in different directions very quickly, and the best way to do it is usually to start your sentences with "But" or "Yet" or—

"Okay, whatever," he said, flashing his great smile. "There's a rule against beginning a sentence with a prepositions—conjunctions, whatever—and you can't break rules." He told me to "take a stab" at an op-ed on the folly of carving out special tax breaks for "green energy" companies or something like that and get it to Rick by the next morning.

A few days later the governor called me. He said something about pay, but so shocked and flattered was I by receiving a call from a sitting governor that I couldn't gather my thoughts sufficiently to negotiate a salary. When I hung up the phone, I was very pleased with myself.

———

I had been working in a library for three long years. I had come back from Scotland in late 2003 with a PhD in English almost in hand, and like most people with freshly attained doctoral degrees in English I had lots of specialized knowledge, high expectations, no job or even job offers, a growing family, and very little money. During those three years working at the library—my chief duty was to attach call number stickers to the spines of books—I had allowed a little anger to creep in. Which was a bitter surprise to me because I had always had a sunny disposition. Then one morning on my walk to work I found myself cursing under my breath for no evident reason. Was I angry at God? At myself for having had such preposterous expectations? Yes in both cases. But it didn't matter; there I was, a doctor making minimum wage performing a low-skill job I conceitedly thought was beneath me. My job title was "annex processor," which was funny because I had long hated the word "process." There's something dishonest about it: processed cheese isn't cheese, process theology isn't theology, process music isn't music, negotiations given the term "peace process" never end in peace, and a "processing fee" is almost by definition a lump of money charged to the customer for no other reason than that the customer is unlikely to notice. So that was me, a "processor."

There was one wonderful thing about that job, though. It was a university library and I could find almost any book I wanted. I'd begun writing essays and reviews for magazines— the *Times Literary Supplement*, the *Weekly Standard*—and having instant access to millions of titles made the research part easy. Moderate success in nonacademic writing led me to wonder if I should drop the idea of an academic job and try for something else entirely, something other than grading papers and going to faculty meetings and turning out articles read by no one but people looking for their own names among the footnotes. I now had a wife and two small children, and I liked where I lived, so getting a job on an oil tanker or joining the military was not an option.

What could I do well? I could write. I had always heard that you can't make a living by writing, but the idea of turning phrases for a living still seemed irresistible. Maybe you couldn't write essays and reviews and novels for a living (I mean, excluding unusual circumstances like writing a break-away best seller or being married to an anesthesiologist or getting a plum job as a writer-in-residence at a university), but you could turn out copy for somebody else. One morning I picked up the newspaper and turned to the opinion page. There was an op-ed by the governor about the state budget then being debated in the General Assembly. It began:

> Bolton, our third son, has always liked the story of the three bears—of the papa, mama and baby bear, and of the porridge being hot, cold and eventually "just right." Work has begun on the state budget, and because that means hot, cold or "just right" now deals with your money, it's worth sizing up whether or not you think things are indeed right in this year's budget.

Without reading any further, I resolved to send him my résumé. I attached a cover letter. It was deferential but terse and said something like "I don't know that much about state politics, but I know how to write, and you need a writer." A few weeks later I found myself in his office talking with him about "brand" and "voice."

For a long time the job of speechwriter had sounded romantic to me. The speechwriter, I felt, was a person whose job it was to put words in the mouths of the powerful, who understood the import and varieties of political language and guided his master through its perils. The speechwriter was a clandestine character; until recently, anyway, you didn't hear much about presidential speechwriters until after the president left office, and even then not much. An air of mystery hangs about the word itself: "Speechwriter" or "speech writer"? One word or two? A speechwriter has all the gratification of being a writer but has political power too, or at least a veneer of it, which was good enough for me.

When I started working for the governor, I didn't do any writing for a week or two. Mainly I just sat behind my desk trying to look busy. At some point the press secretary, Aaron, told me to read through the "op-ed book." This was a giant three-ring binder of photocopies of the governor's published writing over the first four years of his administration. (His second term had begun just a month or two earlier.) Reading the op-ed book would help me get used to the governor's "voice," Aaron told me.

I spent a few hours reading these pieces. It worried me that I didn't hear much of a voice. What I heard was more like a cough. Or the humming of a bad melody, with most of the notes sharp. One sentence stands out in my memory: "This is

10

important not only because I think it ought to be a first order of business, but because it makes common sense."

At that time there were four of us in the press shop or, to speak more correctly, the communications office. Aaron sat at the big desk: he was the communications director, comms director, press secretary, or spokesman. He had been a reporter for one of the regional papers during the boss's first run for governor. He had asked the candidate relentlessly difficult questions and seemed to enjoy it. Aaron's fearlessness, together with his smoking habit, love of rap music, slovenly attire, and youth—he was only twenty-five during that first campaign—all suggested the kind of scorch-and-burn libertarianism that became the governor's brand. The governor-elect (as he became in the fall of 2002) hired Aaron as a speechwriter. That didn't go well. One of Aaron's first contributions was to insert into one of the governor's speeches a glowing reference to Mustafa Kemal Atatürk, an allusion that enraged the state's small but vocal Armenian population. Aaron was far better at talking than writing, and by the time I came on he was the governor's spokesman. He enjoyed arguing for its own sake and did it with a weird combination of conviction and phlegmatic composure. He would get into heated exchanges with other staffers over policy issues, and the whole time his eyes would stay half closed, as if he found the conversation slightly disappointing. Sometimes he would contend with reporters over the phone, the receiver clutched between his head and shoulder, and play video games at the same time. Aaron couldn't be shaken or hurt; he could endure the governor's cruelest and most irrational criticisms as if he'd barely heard them.

There were three other guys in the press office: me, Nat, and an alternating member, which at that time was Mack. Mack was from the Department of Commerce, a cabinet agency. Commerce was on the fifteenth floor of a sleek downtown building adjacent to the State House. The governor had "borrowed" him from Commerce, which was his way of keeping operating costs for the office at about half of what it had been under the previous governor. Mack, who was from Nebraska or one of the Dakotas, seemed angry about being moved from the crisp, spacious offices of the Commerce Department to the governor's cluttered press office. He generally sat with his face sullenly fixed on his computer screen. I believe he had made the understandable but fatal error of interpreting the governor's criticisms of his writing as personal animus. Anyhow he moved on a few months later, and a myth grew up that he had been on the verge of killing someone.

Nat was a Michigander who had found himself in the South through some complicated set of circumstances involving a scholarship. He had a wife and two daughters, as I did, but a fiercer drive to succeed. Nat would usually arrive earlier and stay later than I did, and he was naturally inclined to become more emotionally invested in performing his job well than was healthy. There was a certain dry midwestern intensity about Nat: he laughed without smiling and always seemed to know something you didn't. Later the governor would put him in charge of operations, which meant he was always telling you to do something the governor wanted you to do. He seemed uncomfortable giving direct orders, perhaps because this was the South and southerners don't always say things directly. So he would tell you to do things in awkwardly courteous ways.

"Barton," he might say, trying hard to sound relaxed and friendly, "uh, two questions for you. One, how's your family?"

"They're fine," I would say. "What's the second thing?"

The second thing would of course be the command, which Nat always put in the form of a question: "The Hibernian Society dinner is next month. Could you draft a few toasts for the governor?"

Our office was in the glorious and noble State House, which I reckon is the greatest building in the state, but the press shop itself was a cramped space with the smell of many years of reheated lunches and was difficult to negotiate owing to the great piles of newspapers, magazines, notebooks, and foam board–mounted charts. The walls too were cluttered. Recently there had been a rally outside the State House protesting the governor's veto of a million dollars or so in funding for a bureaucracy called the Arts Commission, and on the wall were two giant placards bearing the words "Keep Funding for the Arts." There were several calendars on the wall, some of them two or three years old. Just over my desk was a picture of the governor, cut from a magazine. He was talking to a small crowd, both his arms extended to one side as if he had been indicating the size of something. Above his head someone had written, "And then a little man about <u>this big</u> came out of the woods and told me to run for governor!"

After about two weeks of my trying to look busy, Nat told me to "take a stab" at a speech. (Members of the press office came naturally to use the governor's own diction, even in casual conversation; sometimes we even peppered our talk with "aahh" and "wwwww.") The speech at which I was to take a stab was an address to one of the state's military brigades, a farewell address before the soldiers left for Afghanistan. I sensed that Nat didn't enjoy writing speeches, that he wanted to move to some other function in the office, and that he had had less than total success as the governor's writer.

The address flowed from my head with no effort at all. Nat told me the governor liked to have three points. Sometimes four, but never two. The speech had to do with honor, sacrifice, and something else, I forget what. It was all fairly predictable, I remember thinking, but I felt I had put the points together with some skill, and I had used two or three quotations that I felt sure would impress the governor: one from a Psalm and another from a speech by Adlai Stevenson, whose biography I had just read.

When you were done writing an address—"talking points" was the general term—you were to place it in the governor's "speech book," the most important of the office's innumerable three-ring binders. Once you put the speech in the speech book, you waited. Usually, Nat said, the governor would come into the press office and tell you he didn't like it and tell you to "take another stab" or to give him "something memorable."

But the governor didn't ask me for any revisions on this first speech.

The day of the speech came, and I listened to it with ears greedy for my own words. As he approached the podium, he walked erect; all his movements seemed smooth and intentional. Once he'd gotten the acknowledgments and thank-you's out of the way, his first words were "As we gather here to send these brave men and women into harm's way, I think it behooves us to remember how fragile life is." I felt a surge of electricity go through me. With the exception of "into harm's way," that's what I had written. I'd chosen the normally ridiculous word "behooves" because it's a military sort of word. He kept going, and it was more or less what I'd written. I felt dizzy. He even used the Adlai Stevenson quote, which I feared might be a stretch.

It wasn't just that they were mostly my words, though. In fact the words themselves weren't particularly memorable, and anyhow the governor didn't sound like a phrase-maker or a wordsmith; he stumbled over a few of the lines and twice pronounced "lest" as "least." It wasn't the words; it was his manner. There was a natural warmth and directness about his presence: the movement of his hands was understated and graceful, his pauses thoughtful rather than awkward, his posture relaxed. Nor was there a hint of the prefab humility you get from most politicians on solemn occasions: the exaggerated tributes to "the brave men and women of the United States military," the body posture that says "This show is about me" even as the mouth discharges panegyrical cant about the character and commitment of others.

The governor knew how to look like he didn't take himself too seriously, as if there had been a time in his life when he didn't.

On the following Monday he called me into a meeting of senior staff. I started to sit, but he told me not to. "Aahh. I just wanted to say, that speech to the Two-eighteenth was fantastic." That was his word, "fantastic." He said he'd used the hard copy of the talk I'd given him, something he said he'd never done before.

For the next forty-eight hours or so, I felt an enormous surge of self-satisfaction. I would soon be indispensable. I would study the questions faced by this great, graceful statesman, and I would suggest to him what he should say. He wouldn't always say what I suggested, but often he would. Someday I would write for the president, maybe. I would be revered for my skills as a fashioner of words.

———

A few days later the governor walked into the press office and said he wanted an op-ed. The topic was the recently concluded legislative session. Nat gave me some guidance on what the governor wanted to say about the session, and I wrote a draft. I gave it to Nat to edit. I stood behind him as he struck and rearranged phrases. I noticed he changed one of my sentences to begin with "Yet."

"He won't like that," I said. "He said he doesn't like beginning sentences with conjunctions."

"He doesn't know 'yet' is a conjunction."

I also noticed Nat alliterating, and mentioned it. He had written "friends of fiscal fecklessness" or "legislative liberality" or something like that. He smiled vaguely. "He hates it. I do it just to make him mad." I asked if he wouldn't mind not doing that, and he agreed to rewrite the phrase. We labored over this little piece for another half hour. The introduction said something about the governor's sons disliking report cards and compared what he had to say about the legislative session to a report card informing parents (taxpayers) where their children (the taxpayers' paid representatives) had succeeded and where they had failed. It was hokey, but only slightly, and it cast the governor in a favorable light: he was a father insisting on accountability at home and in government.

I gave it to him; he said he would read it that night.

The next morning he swung open the great mahogany door of the press office, paper in hand. "Again," he began, clearly dissatisfied. The governor would begin sentences with the word "again" not as a way of calling your attention to something he had said before but as a way of expressing unhappiness. Maybe he had expressed the same opinion on an earlier occasion, but it had been months in the past and was almost certainly said to someone else, not you; or maybe he was referring to the night before, when he had read the piece and mentally criticized it, only you weren't there.

"Again," he said, "this just doesn't sound like me."

"What doesn't sound like you?" I asked.

"It just—it just. I don't know. We're not there. You're not getting the voice."

17

"Can you give me an example?"

"The whole thing. It's just not me. I'll work on this myself and give it to you tomorrow."

The next morning we received his revision. At the top of the page were his initials, signifying (it was explained to me) that no changes were to be made to the document save typographical errors or the most shocking grammatical mistakes. He had rewritten it entirely. Hardly a phrase remained from the draft. I can still recite the opening sentence from memory: "Legislative sessions represent a way of bringing change to our state—and given that our last one ended a few weeks ago, I write to give you my take on what happened and what it means going forward."

I looked at Nat in disbelief. "'Legislative sessions represent a way of bringing change to our state'?"

Nat smiled vaguely as if he had known the outcome beforehand. He told me that "the whole 'new speechwriter' thing" was bound to wear off and that I was now one of the staff. "For two weeks or so you get to be the bright shiny new thing. Then you become—just an old key."

"An old key?"

"Useful occasionally but nothing special. And duplicable. I just made that up. It's actually pretty good."

Aaron was there. It was then that he told me that everyone who worked for this governor had one goal. It wasn't to please him with your superior work, because that would never happen. The goal was to "take away any reason he might have to bitch at you." It was then too that Nat explained that my job wasn't to write well; it was to write like the governor. I wasn't hired to come up with brilliant phrases. I was hired to write what the governor would have written if he had had the time.

"And this is how he writes?"

"Um, yeah," Nat said. "Welcome to hell."

3

The governor had just won reelection to a second four-year term. He had routed his opponent, a gigantic man with an oafish grin who had criticized the governor for failing to "get things done." There was an element of truth in that criticism. The joke about the governor was that he didn't play well with others. Most of the state's legislators hated him; they overrode his vetoes by huge margins. The contrast between him and them was extreme. They spoke with heavy accents; he spoke with a relaxed, somehow aristocratic lilt. They came across as warm and jolly; he was charming but aloof. They were mostly overweight, a few severely so, and physically unprepossessing; he was thin, six feet tall, with deer-like features and sad eyes. They had wives back home and, in many cases, girlfriends in the capital; the governor's wife had a natural, unflashy beauty, and their four well-adjusted young sons lent the family an appearance of decency and strength other politicians long for. The legislators had little regard for ideological differences; apart from the *R*'s and *D*'s after their names, their voting patterns were largely indistinguishable; the majority party exercised near total control of the legislature, and the opposition offered only an occasional squeak in protest, so desperate were its members to hold on to what power and prestige they had. The governor, by contrast, spoke endlessly about ideological differences; again and again he denounced the majority party's—his own party's—reluctance to act on its supposed principles. Their staffers wore seersucker suits with pastel bow ties in the summer and high-quality wool suits the rest of the year; they drove gigantic SUVs and paid for them with six-figure salaries. The governor's staffers were paid little and looked it. Members of the General Assembly enjoyed the perquisites of office and the visible trappings of authority: the catered banquets, the special car tags, the fawning female lobbyists. The tags on the first family's cars were the ordinary ones, and when the governor went to a catered banquet, you'd see him putting boiled shrimp or a couple of deviled eggs into a napkin and stuffing it into his jacket pocket so he wouldn't have to buy dinner on the way home. They named roads and interchanges after themselves; one of the main routes from the capital to the coast, for example, reads like a roll call in the senate. There were never any plans to name anything after the governor.

The governor was famous for his frugality; it was part of the brand. His father, though well off by most standards—he was a heart surgeon in the state's Lowcountry—had prevented his children from enjoying much in the way of luxury. The governor had inherited some wealth, and he'd had a postcollegiate stint at Goldman Sachs and learned to make a good deal more (how I'm not sure). But he inherited his father's parsimonious ways. There were legends about how he had slept on a futon during his days in Congress (he had won his first election in 1994 and served three terms) in order to return his housing allowance to the U.S. Treasury; about how, despite the millions he made in real estate, he had driven the same old Honda for years. In politics, legends are always just legends, and enterprising reporters were always trying to upend those of the governor's frugality. But these attempts usually ended up reinforcing as much of the legend as they contradicted. He hadn't slept on a futon every night, a reporter discovered; often he slept in a Georgetown apartment owned by a friend. But this only emphasized the fact that he had in fact slept on a futon in his office.

The remarkable thing about his reputation for cheapness is that it was true. Or true in spirit. Everybody had a story about the governor's parsimony. I can remember being in the car with him on a sizzling summer afternoon, a security officer driving, the car stopped at a train crossing. While we waited for the train to pass, the governor insisted that the officer turn off the car in order to save gas. Deprived of the air conditioner, we sat for a few minutes while the train took its time. I could see a bead of sweat dropping off the tip of his chin as he talked on the phone and pretended not to notice how miserable he had made himself and us.

Most of his clothing was in a deplorable state. He would not consent to have it dry-cleaned; his staff, and his wife, would occasionally have his shirts and trousers cleaned without his knowledge. He wore only one coat, a navy blazer with one or two missing sleeve buttons, and one pair of trousers, charcoal gray. Both had so many stains that, had they been of a lighter color, their filth would have been revolting. Once I saw inside the collar of one of his white button-up shirts; it was solid brown. Another time he wore the same white shirt, an ink stain on the sleeve, for almost two weeks straight.

It was part of the governor's genius—the remark was commonplace—to turn his mania for saving money into a political asset. His tirades against wasteful government expenditure were delivered with evident conviction. He could not read or hear about the General Assembly dedicating $104,000 for the construction of a green bean museum without visible agitation. When he was shown a newspaper report about a government employee, a university vice president, whose "travel expenses" exceeded the salaries of many of the university's staff, he held the newspaper with one hand and slapped it with the other, as if striking the face of the offender. For a minute he seemed too shaken or angry to speak; he just mumbled, "Bleeding the life out of you people."

The governor's Christmas gifts were a yearly joke. In his congressional days, his wife had bought gifts for the staff, spending a modest sum, $200 or so, according to the legend. When he discovered this, he denounced his wife's improvidence so forcefully that she vowed to leave the task to him. The result was a comedy that, in its way, was more valuable than actual gifts: the governor would regift items that had been given to him by grateful constituents throughout the year. My first year in the office I received a T-shirt advertising a hardware store ("a family business since 1972!"). The next year I received several cans of shoe polish wrapped in cellophane. Mack got a three-year-old jar of preserves. Another staffer received a Christmas ornament bearing the words "Merry Christmas! Love, the Peterkins."

The governor's neurotic cheapness had bigger consequences. One was that most of the staff was under thirty years old. He wanted a tiny staff, paid poorly and prepared to work long hours, which in practice meant young people, mostly unmarried. Sometimes it seemed like a band of kids were in charge of the state. Once, when some of the senior staff were absent, Rick, the chief of staff, remarked that it looked like "Bring Your Kids to Work Day, only without the parents." Another consequence was that you knew you could be let go. It wasn't a typical government job in which you could get lost in the process. There were only about twenty-five of us in the office—half the size of administrations in other small states— and poor performance was obvious to everybody. There was nowhere to hide, no way to settle at the bottom. This was probably a good thing in most respects, but there was something indecent in the way some of us strove, like prisoners in a gulag, to become useful to the master.

I began to think this way after just a few weeks. A month or two in, there were signs that I might not be the writer the governor wanted. Almost certainly wasn't. He hadn't liked any of my op-eds. During those first few months Laura, my wife, told me several times that I needed to start writing badly—badly like him, with clumsy, meandering sentences and openings that seemed calculated to make you stop reading. But I couldn't bring myself to try it.

I don't claim that my writing was brilliant, but the objections he raised were mystifying to me and sometimes totally unreasonable. He would quibble with a harmless phrase and, instead of saying simply that he didn't like it and having me change it or changing it himself, he would fulminate about it and rewrite the entire piece in a fit of irritation. It was almost as if he was afraid that if somebody started writing precisely what he wanted, he'd have no control over what was written. Expressing constant dissatisfaction was perhaps his way of maintaining control. Once, he stormed into the press office, paper in hand, incensed that I had written the words "towns of Lee County." He thought it should have been "towns in Lee County." He walked around to various offices—legislative, policy, law—asking staffers if they thought it sounded right to say "towns of" or "towns in" Lee County.

I tried writing some letters for him. This seemed to go slightly, though only slightly better.

Every great politician has a special discipline, and the governor's was letter writing. The rule was, if anybody said anything favorable about him in the press or anywhere else, that person would get a letter from the governor. Not a form letter: the words had to make it clear that this letter was to this person for this reason. The press office was also tasked with drafting "happy letters"—letters to people who had done something heroic, received awards, or done or achieved something otherwise noteworthy. The governor demanded that large numbers of happy letters be sent out every month, a demand that required us to expand the meaning of noteworthiness. If a citizen of the state had been appointed by the president to a federal regulatory board, that person got a letter. But there were few such occasions, and we were forced to scour the papers for hometown heroes: a local businessman who'd been recognized by the American Red Cross for generosity, an elderly lady who'd been a county librarian for fifty years, a teenager who'd pulled a man from a burning car.

One of the first happy letters I wrote was to a soldier who had been awarded a Purple Heart. I drafted a letter of moderate length written in an informal style with modestly stately diction: not flowery but sufficiently laudatory. I showed him the letter.

"Again," he said, gesturing in a way that signified dissatisfaction. "What did this guy do to get a Purple Heart?"

"He defused roadside bombs."

"I need—you know—something thoughtful, something moving. Just give me something else."

There were several more exchanges between the governor and me over this letter, and they all went about the same way. At last he approved a draft, making only one change. I had written, "the fact that you've risked your life for your country"; he altered it to "risked your life in the service of national duty."

———

It's impossible to attain much success in politics if you're the sort of person who can't abide disingenuousness. This isn't to say politics is full of lies and liars; it has no more liars than other fields do. Actually one hears very few proper lies in politics. Using vague, slippery, or just meaningless language is not the same as lying: it's not intended to deceive so much as to preserve options, buy time, distance oneself from others, or just to sound like you're saying something instead of nothing.

Sometimes, for instance, there would be a matter the governor didn't want to discuss in public, but we knew he'd be asked about it at his next public appearance, or in any case Aaron would be asked about it. Let's say the head of a cabinet agency had been accused by a state senator of running a cockfighting ring. His behavior would fall within executive purview, but since he had not been indicted or even legally accused, he couldn't be fired or forced to resign. Aaron knew the governor would be asked about it at a press conference, so our office would issue a statement to any member of the press who asked about it. "[The senator's] remarks have raised some troubling questions," the statement might say, "and we're looking closely at the situation in an effort to determine whether it merits further investigation by state or local law enforcement. At the same time, we want to avoid rushing to judgment, and we hope all concerned will likewise avoid making accusations in the absence of evidence." This is the kind of statement Aaron would need: one that said something without saying anything. It would get the governor on record without committing him to any course of action. Hence the rhetorical dead weight: "state or local law enforcement" instead of just "law enforcement"; all that about "rushing to judgment" and "making accusations in the absence of evidence," as if anybody needed to be told that. If a reporter asked the governor about it, he could avoid talking about it without having to use that self-incriminating phrase "No comment." "I'd go back to what we've already said on this," he might say, and repeat the gaseous phrases of the statement.

Many people take this as evidence of duplicity or cynicism. But they don't know what it's like to be expected to make comments, almost every working day, on things of which they have little or no reliable knowledge or about which they just don't care. They don't appreciate the sheer number of things on which a politician is expected to have a position. Issues on which the governor had no strong opinions, events over which he had no control, situations on which it served no useful purpose for him to comment—all required some kind of remark from our office. On a typical day Aaron might be asked to comment on the indictment of a local school board chairman, the ongoing drought in the Upstate, a dispute between a power company and the state's environmental regulatory agency, and a study concluding that some supposedly crucial state agency had been underfunded for a decade. Then there were the things the governor actually cared about: a senate committee's passage of a bill on land use, a decision by the state supreme court on legislation applying to only one county, a public university's decision to raise tuition by 12 percent. Commenting on that many things is unnatural, and sometimes it was impossible to sound sincere. There was no way around it, though. Journalists would ask our office about anything having remotely to do with the governor's sphere of authority, and you could give only so many minimalist responses before you began to sound disengaged or ignorant or dishonest. And the necessity of having to manufacture so many views on so many subjects, day after day, fosters a sense that you don't have to believe your own words. You get comfortable with insincerity. It affected all of us, not just the boss. Sometimes I felt no more attachment to the words I was writing than a dog has to its vomit.

It was our job to generate supplies of "language." Once the governor was comfortable with a certain argument or a certain way of stating a position, that became our "language." Language fell under the press office's purview. "Do we have anything on the cigarette tax?" someone from the policy office would ask. "Yeah, we've got language on that." Every week, sometimes every day, some new dispute would have all the attention—tax incentives for corporate retailers, a lawsuit against the Department of Social Services, a bill forcing businesses to verify the immigration status of all their employees—and language was needed for each one. Sometimes you got the feeling that all these fights over policies didn't amount to much more than a lot of words. It was Foucault who held that political power structures were really just a matter of "competing discourses." There's something to that idea, only in my experience nobody controlled anything, and certainly not discourse. Nobody ever won. It felt like a long pitched battle in which there were no victors and only occasional casualties.

Once, when the governor had angered the public education establishment over a funding issue, the office received a barrage of calls chastising him for his "arrogance." Almost all the callers, we began to notice, used that word. Then we realized that most of them were just reading a statement given to them by some advocacy group. I was sitting next to June, the deputy chief of staff, when she took one of these calls. She had heard the statement recited many times already and knew it ended with the words "Please tell the governor to stop his political posturing. We, the voters, are watching." Evidently this caller had stumbled over the phrase "political posturing" and lost her place in the script. So June helpfully added, "You, the voters, are watching?"

"Yes," the caller said.

"Thank you, ma'am," June answered, chewing gum and playing Brick Breaker on her computer. "I'll pass along your message to the governor."

———

Our first task was mastering the language we already had; the second, for me, was developing the capacity to produce it anew. This wasn't going well. I took great pains with my compositions; I groped for just the right word, rearranged sentences to make them strike the ear in just the right way. That's the difficult thing about writing well: you labor for a long time over a single paragraph, as I have this one, and in the end, if you're successful, it looks as if it took no work at all. I anticipated that the governor would sense the difference between what I produced and what my colleagues and predecessors produced.

I did not feel superior to them in other respects. They were far more intelligent and capable than I was and worked faster. They understood the import of complicated policy decisions. They could speak credibly about the differences between competing bills on income tax reduction and the principles underlying each one. They seemed to have a natural and instantaneous grasp of things like labor force growth and global GDP. Yet when they tried to put their understanding into written form, they sounded like morons. Nat was a partial exception here, but even he seemed to think that writing was good only if it sounded grandiose, which to him meant using blistering sarcasm, cute analogies, and of course alliteration.

The governor would ask for an op-ed on some topic and say he wanted it the next morning. Ordinarily you'd have to know a lot about labor force growth to write an op-ed on it, but I didn't. The policy shop would provide the relevant facts and analysis; my job was to shape those into eight hundred words of readable English. I would spend most of the night rewording phrases for maximum effect, perfecting transitions, scouring my mind for just the right metaphors, making the discussion of policy sound authoritative but not wonkish, and giving the last paragraph that sting that makes an op-ed memorable.

And he'd hate it. Once, the door of the press office flew open and the governor, paper in hand, started to explain to me why what I had written wasn't right. "Again."

After experiencing a few seconds of what looked like

unbearable frustration, he summoned the words to explain what galled him. "I would never say, 'the extent to which.'"

"So let's say something different."

"But my point is, you've got to know your audience. The mechanic in Greenwood doesn't go around talking about things being 'the extent for which.'"

"The extent to which."

"Whatever. My point is, always know your audience. I'll work on this tonight."

When the op-ed came back to us, it began, "As the old saying goes, the first step to getting out of a hole is to quit digging. I think this certainly applies to the mountain of debt now facing our country."

"Is it a hole, or is it a mountain?" I asked after the governor had walked out. I must have developed a reputation for pedantry over matters of language because Aaron asked me to shut up.

It helped to tell my wife about these episodes. We laughed at them. But they made me unhappy.

⚘ MY LIST

I sat at my desk, ready to hear about how another of my op-eds was all wrong. This time the governor himself didn't tell me; Aaron did. He had just come from a "hand-off." The governor would call senior staff into his office and "hand off" miscellaneous pieces of paper to them—articles ripped from newspapers, business cards, his own handwritten notes, drafts of letters or op-eds, sometimes nothing more than a tiny yellow sticky note. He had usually written something on each of them: "Show to R" or "When jobs #s?" or just "?" In the case of written products generated by our office, he would sometimes draw a Δ at the top. This meant he wanted it changed but couldn't say how or why. Once he gave me a shred of paper that looked as if it had been ripped from an envelope; he'd scribbled the words "kraut gdp" on it. This meant he wanted me to find an op-ed in which the columnist Charles Krauthammer discussed world debt relative to GDP, or something like that. Another time I saw him give Paul, the head of the policy office, a draft of a policy letter written by one of our staffers; across the top of it the governor had written the words "Written by 6 year old?"

Staffers came out of hand-offs holding a pile of papers, trying to remember what the governor wanted done about each one. Aaron pulled from his pile an op-ed I'd written the day before. "He hated this. He said it was too strident, and he wants more 'cool stuff.' Sorry, man. Oh yeah, and he said he would never say—let's see, where is it?—right here. He would never say 'And it's easy to see why.' I don't know why that hacked him off so bad."

I sat staring blankly at my draft—the governor had scrawled a giant question mark across the first page—wondering how dispensable I was. I had been there only a few months. Later in the day Aaron motioned for me to step into the conference room. It felt ominous. He asked me how things were going and other questions one might ask a fairly recent hire. Then he said, "The governor's thinking of bringing in a new writer."

I just sat there trying to look placid.

"It's not that you're a bad writer."

"I know," I snapped. Then, more slowly, "I know that I'm not a bad writer."

It was just that he wasn't sure I could write like him. You might be a great writer, Aaron explained, but if you can't write like he wants you to, you're gone. He had told the governor to hold off and give me more time.

"Thanks, Aaron."

I brooded about this for a day or two and then discussed it with my wife. This time I gave real thought to her counsel to write badly. One of the governor's op-eds published about this time, one he himself had written in defense of a nonprofit group he'd started a few months before, contained these sentences:

> Unfortunately, some like Speaker Bobby Harrell* have reacted negatively—depicting it as an effort to give a punch in the nose. It is not that. It is about friends across this state caring enough about the importance of change that they will invest time, money and effort in bringing it about.

"An effort to give a punch in the nose," full stop. "Friends across this state caring enough about the importance of change"—as if they cared not about the abstract concept of "change," which was nonsensical enough, but about its "importance." I felt confident that if I had written these words and given them to the governor, he would have fired me on the spot. He knew bad writing when he saw it, except when he was the author. Something about its provenance in his own

---

* Bobby Harrell, speaker of the house, was the most powerful man in the state house. He wielded his power like a cudgel; nobody in the legislature liked or crossed him. He didn't look the part at all, curiously: a little man with hardly any expression in his face. I read somewhere that the human face contains fifty-three muscles. Harrell looked as if he had only about ten.

brain made him see mellifluous perfection where everybody else saw the awkward platitudes of a high school term paper.

My job wasn't all bad. To the governor I was a liability, but to the rest of the staff I'd become an authority. Almost instantly I'd acquired the reputation of a grammarian. Nearly every day my phone would ring and someone would ask, "Is it 'none is' or 'none are'?" or "Can you use 'impact' as a verb?" or "Do you capitalize 'judicial branch'?" At first I tried to respond with nuanced explanations about how this usage was once considered incorrect but had become so common that educated people now use it routinely, or about how that rule was useful as a guide although it could be broken in some circumstances. But I sensed impatience. All my questioners wanted to know was what was right and what was wrong. They didn't care what was generally accepted or defensible; they wanted to know what they should say in order not to sound like ignoramuses. Someone once called to ask me if "alleve" was a word. This young woman was transcribing a letter the governor was dictating; when she questioned the word, he told her to ask me.

"I don't think so. It's a pain medicine, isn't it? Aleve, A-L-E-V-E."

"That's what I told him, but he swears it's a word."

"You look it up in the dictionary?"

"It's not in there."

"He must be thinking of 'alleviate.'"

"He wants to use 'alleve.'"

"He's confusing 'relieve' and 'alleviate.'"

"He wants 'alleve.'"

"Well, give it to him, I guess. But tell him he needs to

get permission from whoever owns Aleve. Maybe put a little trademark sign beside it."

It was around this time that I got the idea—or maybe I was asked to do it, but I think it was my idea—to help transcribe the governor's dictated letters. His personal assistant, Lewis, brought me an ancient dictation machine, a tape of fifteen or so letters, and a pair of headphones. I typed them out as best I could and gave the document to Lewis for editing. Over the next four or five months I transcribed well over a thousand letters from the governor. It was tedious work. Most of them began with the words "I just wanted to write." The governor wrote letters to almost everyone he met, especially, though not exclusively, those whom he perceived to be important or in some way influential. Some of them were extremely short. "This is a letter to Bill Dixxon," he'd say into the Dictaphone. "Dear Bill, I just wanted to write and say how much I enjoyed being with you over the weekend. You've got a great way about you, and I did enjoy the chance to know you a little better. I hope our paths cross again soon. Until then, take care. Sincerely." Some of them were longer but still routine: expressions of appreciation for invitations or gifts, notes of condolence for lost relatives or of happiness for job promotions he had read about in *Barron's* or some local business magazine. Others were longer and had to do with governmental affairs.

A few were to his family. He would write long letters to his sons about how much he enjoyed watching their track meets and baseball games, telling them what Calvin Coolidge said about perseverance. Sometimes you'd find out who the governor had met or been with while he was out of the office.

"This is a letter to Colin Powell"; "This is a letter to Charlie Rose"; "This is a letter to Brian Williams."

He wrote so many letters that occasionally he would forget the name of the person he was writing to. "This is a letter to what's-his-name," he'd begin. "Jeane will know his name, ask Jeane." Jeane was our senate liaison and someone who knew nearly everyone. "Dear whoever," he would continue, "I just wanted to let you know how sorry I was to hear about your dad. I remember losing my dad when I was seventeen, and all I can say is it wasn't easy. Please know you'll be in our prayers over the coming weeks and months." I wondered if the governor would pray for somebody whose name he couldn't remember. Would he tell God to ask Jeane?

Occasionally he'd forget almost every relevant piece of information. "This is a letter to what's-his-name. Ask Jeane. Dear whatever, I just wanted to write and say I appreciated—whatever it was—he sent something, a box of pecans or something—I hope to see you soon down at wherever—he has a house somewhere, we were there last year. Ask Jeane. Please pass along a hello to whatever his wife's name is. Take care. Sincerely." I spent many hours trying to figure out what should take the place of the "whatevers" and "wherevers."

After several weeks of transcribing his letters I started to recognize stock phrases. His syntax became familiar, and I could anticipate certain ungainly phrases before he said them. It was like listening to twelve-tone music: you had to force yourself to do it, but after a while you could discern some charmless patterns, and even like them in a perverse kind of way.

To people he had met who had impressed him for some

reason—and he wrote letters to all such people—he would say, "You've got a great way about you." He began many sentences with "given the fact": "Given the fact that we'll be in Europe in June, I thought there might be a chance we could meet in Prague." There were maladroit sentence lengtheners, intended to make sentences look more consequential or thoughtful than they were: "none other than" ("The dinner was none other than fabulous"; "Failing to address this problem would be none other than disastrous"), "in your direction" ("I wanted to send a thank-you in your direction"), "over the weeks and months ahead" ("You'll be in our prayers over the weeks and months ahead"). Hours of listening taught me to divine the reasons for his choice of words. "Indeed," for example, had a number of purposes, all of them more or less inapt. Sometimes he dropped it into hackneyed phrases in order to let his reader know that he knew they were hackneyed but that they were true anyhow: "We're mortgaging our children's future" would become "We're indeed mortgaging our children's future," and those who failed to learn from history were "indeed" doomed to repeat it. Sometimes "indeed" served to separate words that sounded awkward together. Every writer encounters this problem; you can't use the words "voters voting in the next election" without sounding odd. A careful writer would find a new way of saying it; the governor's solution was to write "voters indeed voting in the next election." I remember a press release I drafted for him in which he added the sentence "Jefferson and the founding fathers indeed founded this nation on the notion of limited government."

Eventually I began to compile a list of his favorite words and phrases. Here is one version of the list I still have with me:

PHRASES

Given the fact that

toward that end

in which you operate

the level of

both . . . and frankly

goes well beyond

the way you live your life

in this regard (in this regard it's worth . . .)

in many ways

none other than

this larger (this larger notion/ idea)

for that reason

in large measure

as a consequence

more than anything

in my direction

nonetheless (small but nonetheless significant sign)

over the weeks and months ahead

speaks volumes

NOUNS

range (a range of)

host (a host of, whole host of)

admiration (usu. profound admiration)

pearls (of wisdom)

ADJECTIVES, ADVERBS

remarkable

incredible (working incredibly hard)

inevitably

frankly

awfully

larger

disturbingly so, especially so

amazingly

considerable (very considerable)

fabulous

dire

VERBS

present

impress (impressed me)

admire (admire the fact that)

highlight

underscore

OTHER

inasmuch

whereby

This collection summarizes the governor's character as well as any biography could, though I reckon only I can see that. Its terms are plain and practical, but they're boring, and most of them are slightly awkward. Some are lazy: the only reason to say something "speaks volumes"—"The fact that you refused to give up speaks volumes about your character"—is because you want the credit for making a large claim without bothering to find words to make it.

Any time I was asked to write a letter or an op-ed, I'd have this list in front of me. Sometimes, instead of consulting it to help me put an idea into the right words, I would get my ideas from the list itself. If I didn't know how to begin, say, an article for the Chamber of Commerce magazine, I'd just write "in which you operate." I'd stare at it for a few minutes, then I might begin, "This administration has always operated on the principle that government doesn't have all the answers." Or I would write "in large measure" and wait. Then it would come to me: "The government structure given to us by our state's constitution is in large measure a throwback to the days just after Reconstruction, and it's for that reason our administration has taken the stand it has." Eventually, in the case of op-eds, he would change nearly everything I wrote, but if it contained enough of his own syntax, he at least wouldn't be outraged, and sometimes he'd leave it alone.

Once, I heard him tell a reporter, "I write all my own stuff." He said it with conviction, and I was standing beside him. At first I was appalled; he knew I wrote his "stuff," or a lot of it. Later, though, I reflected that when he read language written deliberately in his own strange voice, he felt he had written it. And in a sense he was right.

One day he burst into the press office, as usual criticizing something I'd written. "Again, I would never write this."

I looked at it and didn't recognize it. I told him I hadn't written it; he had.

He paused and looked at it more closely. "Are you sure?" he asked.

"Yes, I'm sure," I said. But I wasn't.

5

LETTERS

One Sunday night in February, Shelby, the governor's scheduler, called me at home to tell me I would be traveling with the governor on Monday to three small towns. These would not be a day's round of the usual press conferences, which would have taken place in the larger cities with bigger media markets, but a series of fifteen-minute "talks" to local businesses. Each stop would involve a small crowd—as many as a hundred, as few as almost nobody—and two or three local journalists. The talk involved three bills the governor wanted to see passed in the legislature: one on drunk driving penalties, one on the amalgamation of two state agencies, and one on the state budget.

I was to get the day's schedule from Lewis, who would

explain my duties. These sounded complex: Motion to the governor "five minutes" when you have ten minutes before you have to leave. If you wait until you've got only five minutes, Lewis explained, it'll take him ten minutes to get away from the crowd, and when he finds out he's five minutes late he'll blame you. Remember, he said, you've got to be the bad guy. If someone's hogging the governor's attention, he doesn't want to be the one to break it off. You've got to step in and say something like "Governor, I'm so sorry, but we've really got to make the next appointment." I was to shadow him, but not walk too closely, especially if there weren't very many people around him. Lewis said more than once, "He hates the entourage look."

Was anyone traveling with us? It was just me, the governor, and a member of the security detail.

Richard Mitchell, the comptroller general, I learned, would be at each stop. Mitchell was one of the governor's allies. "But unfortunately," Lewis said, "he won't be in the car with you." I wondered what he meant by "unfortunately."

On the way to the first event, the governor read the *Wall Street Journal*. When he was done, he folded it up and threw it into the backseat—that is, at me. I had heard that if you sat in the backseat when he was in the front, the governor would throw things at you. Not at you, exactly, just into the backseat. But he wasn't trying not to throw things at you, either. When he was working, staffers existed—physically, literally—only insofar as they could aid him. In one sense it was impossible not to admire the man's ability to fix his attention so exclusively on whatever he was doing. Still, it was unnerving to realize that, to him, at that moment, you were a nonentity; you weren't.

This was the first of three days of these talks, and first days of anything usually went badly. The governor always needed a few practice runs before he was comfortable with what he was saying. He would thumb through the talking points and inevitably find something he disliked or some question un-asked or unaddressed. When this happened he would ask the nearest staffer a question you couldn't answer. Silence was the worst possible response. It suggested to him that you were try-ing to make something up.

"What was the Second Injury Fund?"

"I don't know. But I'll call Stewart and find out."

Having talked to Stewart—at that time deputy chief of staff for policy—you would try to tell the governor what the Second Injury Fund was, but he would ask another question you weren't able to answer, and soon the superfluity of your role as mediator would become apparent and he'd grab the phone from you. Stewart knew everything, and the governor depended on him a great deal, but for reasons I never quite grasped he never wanted to talk to Stewart directly unless he had to. Perhaps it made his dependence on his deputy too ob-vious.

The talks that day didn't go well. Not that the people hosting them cared. Owners of little stores and repair shops in small towns were happy to have the governor there and didn't care what he said. But I didn't have the knack for manag-ing him. I couldn't bring myself to interrupt his conversations with "five minute" warnings, with the result that we left each stop ten, fifteen, or twenty minutes behind schedule—which enraged him more each time.

He hadn't warmed to his talk yet. One of his points had to do with the difference between certain lawmakers' bold rhetoric on tax reform and their tendency to weaken reform legislation when given the chance. He wanted to say, "So we'll see if the juice was worth the squeeze," meaning, I think, we'll see if it was worth counting on their stated intentions. The expression didn't precisely fit, and he made it worse by repeatedly reversing "juice" and "squeeze." "We'll see if the squeeze was worth the juice." Everyone listened respectfully, but I thought I saw two machinists exchange looks of perplexity.

Mitchell was there to talk about transparency in government. He believed, with some evidence, that state lawmakers were using parliamentary measures to hide unnecessary and, in some cases, unethical appropriations. He seemed to enjoy himself. At each stop he would draw a theme from the physical surroundings. The first stop was a warehouse in which the steel frames of small boats were built. "It's funny we're here where boats are made," Mitchell began, with his characteristically warm smile, "because our ship of state is sinking in a sea of red ink."

This was around the time when speculation about the governor's chances on a national ticket began to circulate. For a variety of reasons, most of them negative (he didn't have the liability of so-and-so; as a state rather than a federal officeholder he had no record on such-and-such), he was among those thought to be attractive vice presidential candidates.

"Are you interested in the vice presidency, Governor?" a reporter would ask, knowing he couldn't answer yes or no. Over the next several months he went through a series of responses. On this occasion he was experimenting with the unhappy analogy of being struck by lightning. "That's very flattering, but it's all just surreal," he would say. "It's so unlikely. But if lightning does strike, I'd be lying if I said I'd hang up the phone." Saying yes or no to a lightning strike didn't sound right. But at first he couldn't even get the lightning line right. "If that lightning bolt strikes," he would say, or "If that lightning bolt falls in my direction," or "If that ball of lightning ever does come my way."

We were at the third stop, an establishment that sold high-end cookware, when my phone vibrated.

"Hey, it's Aaron."

"We're in the middle of the event here," I whispered.

"When it's over, tell the governor Jakie's calling for an investigation over the NGA thing." "Jakie" was Jake Knotts, a state senator and a venomous critic of the governor.

"Investigation?"

"Yeah."

"Investigation of what?"

"Just tell him it's about the NGA thing. He'll know what you mean."

"It's funny we're here beside all these cooking pots," Mitchell was saying, gesturing to a display of Dutch ovens.

"What's 'the NGA thing'?" I whispered to Aaron.

"Just tell him Jakie's calling for an investigation over the NGA grant."

"... this state has been cooking the books for a long time."

"What NGA grant?"

"He'll know what you're talking about. Jakie's on the floor right now. It's already on the AP wire."

"Knotts, calling for an investigation," I repeated to Aaron. "About cooking the books."

"No. About the NGA grant."

"Sorry. NGA grant."

When we got into the car, I said to the governor, "Aaron called a minute ago. Knotts is on the floor of the senate calling for an investigation." Suddenly I couldn't recall why. All I could remember was that it wasn't about cooking the books.

"What's he want to investigate?"

"He—Aaron—seemed to think you'd know," I lied.

"I don't know. I'm asking you. Why's Knotts calling for an investigation?"

"I don't know."

"Okay," the governor said fiercely, "you just told me somebody's saying there should be an investigation. Investigation of what? Of me? And you don't know why? I'm asking. You don't know?"

"It was in the middle of the press conference and I didn't get the details."

"Okay, so you're going to tell me I'm being investigated, but you're not going to tell me why?"

"Oh! I know. The NGA grant."

"What about the NGA grant?"

"Now that I don't know. Aaron said you'd know."

"Again, I don't know. I'm asking you."

This went on for three or four minutes. I wondered why he didn't just pick up his phone and call Aaron for the details, or tell me to. Later I would realize that he knew everything about it already and that this was his way of coping with distressing news. He wasn't trying to demean me, but when he was anxious, he needed somebody to berate, and you were nearby and a staffer you were that somebody. Being belittled was part of the job. It created a weird camaraderie among the staff: we would relay the latest episode and compare it to the "classic" ones of former times. "Nothing tops the time he lectured Lewis for getting the wrong burrito," someone would say, and the stories would all be retold again.

The next morning in the office the air felt tense. When I arrived, the governor was already there, which was unusual. (Ordinarily he would arrive at ten or ten-thirty.) Aaron was walking up and down the governor's wing of the State House, from the press shop to the governor's office, pen and tablet in hand, as if he were waiting tables.

I gathered from Nat that the bustle had to do with Knotts's accusations. I read the reports from the AP and *The State*—the first I knew about any of it. A year before, the National Governors Association had had its annual meeting in Charleston. The governor had done a few fund-raisers to help offset the cost to the taxpayers, and that money included a $150,000 grant from the state. As it turned out, the funds raised had exceeded what was needed by a substantial figure. The governor had put the excess in the account of Reform Alliance, a nonprofit advocacy group he had founded a year before. Actually "group" is probably an exaggeration; as far as I know it was just a bank account and maybe a staffer and a laptop. The question was whether the money he raised for the NGA, which included governors from both parties, belonged to the state. If it didn't, he could presumably do whatever he wanted with the unspent portion. If it did, he was guilty of diverting state funds to what could almost be called his personal account, "a potentially serious offense," wrote editorialists who didn't know whether or not it was serious.

Aaron had already put out a statement on the matter, but reporters were calling for more in the way of explanation and response. After a few months of listening to Aaron on the phone, I could tell when he felt at ease with the official position and when he didn't. When it was clear that we had the stronger argument, he sounded both warm and utterly self-confident—not an easy trick. But when our argument was in any way lacking, there was just a hint of uncertainty in his answers, a brittleness. His voice would go up an octave, and his phrasing became uncharacteristically bland and formulaic.

He was adept with reporters, with whom he communicated mainly by phone. He knew each one as a salesman knows his clients, and he always returned their calls. There were some he would treat tenderly, as if worried they might turn against him at some slight provocation; others he would hound into submission or shout at the way a baseball manager shouts at an umpire, not in order to change his mind but to register a grievance in the hope of better treatment next time.

There were two or three reporters with whom he would contend as with an ornery sibling. Chief among these was Donald Hatfield of the AP. When Donald called, the two would almost immediately descend into an appalling verbal brawl over factual claims. A few reporters he thought mendacious or stupid. Some of these he would humor, owing to the prestige of their employers. His phone would ring, and, seeing the caller's number, he'd shout insults—"Oh, Cecil Sanderson, I don't want to talk to you, you bastard"—just before picking up the phone and saying, in a sunny, welcoming voice, "Governor's Office, this is Aaron. Oh hey, what's happening, Cecil?"

The reporter calling this morning was Barry Clarke of the *Post and Courier*. "He's the victim of his last conversation," Aaron would say about him; he meant that Clarke took as fact whatever he'd been told by the person he'd spoken to before you. In this instance Clarke had spoken first to someone from an advocacy group who had said categorically that the governor had broken the law. By that morning our legal office could make a cogent argument that transferring the funds to a nonprofit was not illegal, yet Aaron could not shake Barry's confidence in the soundness of the storyline. The anguish in his voice was difficult to listen to.

"This is the end," Nat said to me quietly. "This is it. We're done."

Nat, I sensed, liked the feeling of impending collapse. But he was young, so an overmastering sense of irony kept him from earnestness of any kind.

"This is it, man," he said. "Improper use of funds. We're done. Start sending out résumés."

Mack turned from his computer screen. "You really think so?" It was the first thing Mack had said in a couple of days.

"This won't last past today," I said. "You get impeached for taking money for yourself, not for 'redirecting' it into some stupid nonprofit."

"Except that 'some stupid nonprofit' and the governor are the same thing," Nat growled.

"Jakie's a sleazebag," Mack said, turning back to his computer screen. "It doesn't matter what he says." That was almost true. Jakie was a nefarious bigot and everybody knew it. You felt even he knew it. But he was also a state senator. Somebody turned on the television to watch the senate. One of the members was explaining that his bill would offer tax credits to anyone who refurbishes an abandoned rice mill. "There are so many of these ol' abandoned rice mills in my district," the member was saying. "Wouldn't it be great to encourage businesses to use them, to make them look purdier [prettier]?" It was an open secret among lawmakers and State House staffers that the brother-in-law of the member introducing the bill was then wanting to start a business in an abandoned rice mill. Somebody had suggested the governor veto the bill and include the word "dizzy" in the veto letter. Dizzy was the brother-in-law's name.

The senator finished his plea after a windy explanation, the vote was taken, and the bill passed on second reading by a wide margin.

"The Knottsie's next," said Gil, a policy advisor. "Knottsie," pronounced "Nazi," was his name for Jakie Knotts. Gil was known for his inventive jokes at the expense of legislators. ("Know how to spell 'McConnell?'" he once asked me. "Two *c*'s, two *n*'s, two *l*'s, and two faces.") Gil was pretty evidently in the wrong line of work; his research was sometimes inaccurate, his writing could be incoherent, and his opinions on policy matters seemed unmoored to any principle: one minute he would loudly proclaim support for legislation allowing law enforcement officers to take DNA samples at the point of arrest, and the next he would argue for the legalization of drugs. Everybody liked Gil. He was frequently wrong, but you had the feeling he knew this about himself. He often stretched his arms and back while he talked, as if he'd just awoken from a nap.

Several staffers were now gathered around the television in our office, watching the senate. One of these was Stewart. He had been with the boss since his congressional days and took this longevity as license to refer to the governor in fantastically demeaning terms. This had the strange effect of boosting morale, inasmuch as it gave you comfort to know that ill feelings toward the boss didn't signify incompetence or disloyalty or an inability to get along or even personal dislike. In appearance Stewart was not prepossessing: every day he wore a gigantic charcoal suit—in those days he was thirty pounds overweight—with a cheap white shirt and a drab tie; his haircuts were usually bad, and the roundness of his face gave him a boyish aspect that was only partially camouflaged by an intermittent beard and tiny wire-frame glasses. But he was utterly indispensable; he understood every policy question the administration had ever faced, and he could explain the import of each one in overarching terms or in detail. Although he had a fierce temper (several of his assistants had fled in tears and never returned), Stewart had a way of cheering everybody up. He had a penchant for vaguely inappropriate humor and laughed with a great baritone tremolo; sometimes in a convulsion of laughter he flung himself violently backward in his chair and you feared he might fall and hurt himself. His jeremiads were notorious. When an adversary criticized the governor, Stewart would emit long streams of profane and grammatically flawless invective in defense of the administration. By the end, you wondered what reason anyone could have for criticizing policies so obviously reasonable. After a year or so it started to seem improbable that we were so consistently and wholly right about everything, but even then Stewart's jeremiads offered warm reassurance that we were basically, if not always wholly, in the right.

At a time like this we needed Stewart around, and I was glad he was there. Aaron casually mentioned that the governor had returned the money.

"Returned the money?" somebody asked.

Yes, Stewart said. That morning the governor had transferred the money out of Reform Alliance's account and put it in the state's General Fund.

Nat wanted to know why.

"For the sake of appearances. He hasn't done anything wrong, but just to be completely above board, he wanted to put the money into the General Fund."

Nat rejected that explanation as "press secretary crap" and pointed out correctly that when you return something in a situation like this, you look guilty. Aaron said he'd told the boss that, and so had Stewart, "but that's what he wanted to do."

Stewart: "You know he's always got to go further than any other politician would. He's got to be lily white, Nat. He's incorruptible."

Nat: "Oh, that's great, now he looks like a crook. He didn't do anything wr—. Why would you—? Why didn't somebody—?" It was a sign of Nat's displeasure when he spoke in fragments. It was his way of saying things that couldn't be said without actually saying them; in this case he was saying that Stewart and Aaron had countered the governor's intention with insufficient force. He was saying they'd been cowards, and both of them knew he was saying it. I gathered from their silence that they knew he was right.

"The Knottsie's getting up," announced Gil.

We watched as Knotts lifted himself out of his chair and leaned his belly against his desk. Senators spoke with hand-held microphones, and Knotts liked to put his almost into his mouth, so you couldn't always understand what he was saying. He asked the senate president to allow some arcane parliamentary move, was granted permission to speak, and began. "Mistah President, I wauna take up this ishah of the govnah's abuse of powah. I wauna stress at the beginning that what we're taukin' about ain't juss a matter of some"—his mouth stretched open, baring his teeth—"technicality."

"He's getting warmed up, boys," Gil said.

"What we're taukin' about is a alleged crime. Issa crime to take money from the state. He says, 'Oh, but I put it back.' Mistah President, our jails is full o' people who wish they could put back the money they stole and go free. Our jails is full o' people who wish they could juss put it back, juss undo everythang."

"I knew he—," Nat said.

"Mistah President, this is typical of this govnah. Thass what I been trying to tell y'all. This is a man who thinks he's above the law. We got serious problem in this state. We got unemployment, we got crime, we got all kinds o' problem. The lass thing we need is a govnah who thinks he's above the law. That's just makin' our problem worse."

The governor walked into the office. You could sense everyone's disappointment; we were just starting to enjoy the speech. When the governor was there you didn't feel the same liberty to crack jokes; you felt obliged to look busy and laugh nervously any time he attempted a bit of humor.

"The textile warehouse bill passed," somebody said.

"Big surprise," the governor said. "How many votes on our side?"

"Two."

"That's a disgrace."

"For too long," Knotts was saying, "this state's been gettin' the short end of the totem pole."

"Anybody besides Knotts talking?" the governor asked.

"No," Stewart said. "Well, there's a rumor that McKinney is going to join him, but I don't see that happening."

"Who's McKinney?"

Stewart looked at the governor with feigned disappointment. "Governor, really?" Stewart liked to remind the governor of his omniscience in strategically important matters such as past policy positions and the names and voting patterns of legislators. I had the feeling the governor didn't like this, or at least didn't like Stewart's calling attention to it in front of other staffers, but it was true and he needed to be reminded of it. I couldn't understand why he thought he could get away with not knowing the names of lawmakers—do other governors simply neglect to memorize their names?—but in the end it would cost him.

"Okay, I get it, Stewart. So who's McKinney?"

"Really? You actually don't know who Senator McKinney is?"

"Stewart, I get it." I thought I saw a look of irritation in his eyes. Then he said placidly, "I know who McKinney is. Is he important or not?"

". . . this govnah's tryin' to hang his hat on our coat hanger."

"Glenn McKinney," sighed Stewart. "Been in the Senate for like twenty years. Though, granted, he doesn't do much."

"So is he important? Is he going to sway what's-his-name to vote with him?"

". . . now he's got his lawyer, this hand-picked puppet, doin' his talkin' for him."

"No, I wouldn't say he's important. And there's not going to be a vote. This is a rhetorical exercise."

The governor did know the names of the important legis-lators, and one or two unimportant ones from his own part of the state. But he didn't care who they were. They sensed this, and it enraged them.

"Let me know if anything happens," he said, and walked out.

The next morning, the *Herald* and several other re-gional papers ran an eight-hundred-word op-ed by Senator Jake Knotts. It began, "'Methinks he doth protest too much.' There is great wisdom in that ancient Shakespearian line." Gil walked into our office for a few high-fives.

"Did you see the Knottsie's piece this morning? Wonder who wrote that intro for him. I bet he's never even heard of Othello." Still, you couldn't dislike Gil.

The governor had phoned in (he was speaking some-where in the Lowcountry) and told me to "churn out some surrogate letters," meaning letters to the editor that would appear to be sent by one of our supporters but would be written by me. This is a common practice in politics: cal-culated advertisements made to look like spontaneous out-bursts.

I should explain that it had become my duty to respond to favorable letters to the editor published in the state's newspa-pers. These included letters in the three major dailies as well as all the smaller papers, of which there were around twenty that I knew of. It was one of the governor's unshakable con-victions that letters to the editor had great influence on public opinion. Nat, whose duty it had been before I came, had once tried to tell the governor that letters to the editor are so poorly written, cranky, and consistently illogical that even positive ones are a net liability. But the boss did not believe it. Print had the power to sway, in his view, no matter what the print said. I think he was right.

I was to monitor letters in order to respond to those that complimented the governor in some way. Apart from the time this consumed, it was an easy task, once you had his angular style firmly in your head. For almost all of them, you'd begin with something like "Dear so-and-so: I read your letter in *The State* and just wanted to thank you for writing as you did." Then you'd restate the thrust of the letter, or the part of it that the governor would appreciate, usually including the word "indeed," and then reaffirm the original letter's opinion in a way that made it clear to the recipient that this wasn't a form letter but a personal expression of gratitude. "The unpaid-for political promises made by state government over the last number of years have indeed reached a crisis point, and I do appreciate you making your voice heard on that front. Take care. Sincerely."

Once you knew what sorts of letters the governor would respond to—all that praised him specifically and also many that took positions with which he agreed—it was a pretty easy task. It wasn't a waste of time, either, from the point of view of politics. People who write letters to the editor believe that the thoughts they took pains to put into words are insightful and original, and they are eager to see that opinion confirmed. The state, the nation, the world is in some respect ill-arranged, and they feel they have knowledge that can set it right. They want to see their words demolish the strongholds of prejudice and

ignorance by force of logic. Of course very few letters to
the editor come anywhere near coherence. Mostly they're
fragments of platitudes basted with the rhetoric of outrage.
I used to clip the best ones. I kept a folder full of them;
the one I have before me now deals with a subject about
which I no longer have any recollection, but it's typical in
its white-hot incomprehensibility. "This attitude is ludi-
crous, to say the least," the letter concludes (on the letters
page even the strongest words are qualified with "to say
the least"), "with both sides sounding like perennial fence
sitters. As for this situation they need simply to know the
difference between right and wrong. They, like so many
in this community, appear to be waiting for the next shoe
to fall, trusting only in their instincts so as to land on the
'right' side of the fence." You wouldn't think these letter
writers took much time to compose their broadsides, but
you'd be wrong. And their authors are extremely eager for
their thoughts to be well received. When they discover that
the governor himself profited from their wisdom, they're
grateful. Some of them would reply to him, thanking him
for writing and saying they would frame his letter. These
people, already disposed to like him, would now revere
him. Enlisted soldiers became warriors.

Some of them, as a result of the governor's gratitude,
would write more letters to newspapers. I kept a running
list of their names so that when they wrote a second letter
I could thank them for "another" or for their "latest" letter.
One of these, I remember, was somebody named Larry Jones
II. He wrote so many letters, all of them ecstatically praising

the governor's virtues and heaping ridicule on his adversaries, that after a time I had to stop responding to them lest it appear improbable that the governor himself was responding. Jones II once wrote a letter to the governor asking him to attend some sort of society gathering where men would talk about political philosophy and smoke cigars. He got a polite regret, or maybe—I forget—no reply at all. We would hear from him again.

There was a sense of surreptitiousness about this, as there usually is inside political offices. You always feel you're doing something that, if known, would scandalize somebody. That's what makes it fun, especially if you're young. But my conscience bothered me about the letters; it bothered me even more when I realized the governor didn't read half the letters I wrote for him. Though it was a good sign that he had started to trust me, at least with low-level stuff like letters, it seemed wrong that he wasn't even reading some of them. Even now there may be letters framed, prominently displayed in offices and living rooms, that the governor neither composed nor read.

I asked June, the deputy chief of staff, about it.

"He was brought up in the South," she said. "That's what you do."

Here's what I think she meant. The governor had been raised (as I had) to believe that if someone did something for which you were grateful, you bore an obligation to express that gratitude in writing. Mother made you write a thank-you note after your uncle took you duck hunting or after you had received a sweater from Grandmother. It didn't matter if your feet were frozen and you didn't fire a shot or if the sweater didn't fit and made you look like a girl; you wrote the thank-you letter. These loyal constituents had done something similar. They had in some small way provided empirical evidence that average people liked what the governor was doing. It was impossible for him to respond to all these signals of favor, or even to a majority of them. The letters I composed were what he would have expressed if he were able to do it himself. Nor, after I had talked to June about it, did I let it bother me that there were electoral benefits to these responses. It was his habit; he was a politician; why should he spurn a habit just because it advanced his career?

I didn't respond to hostile letters; the governor said he didn't want to get "tangled up" with people who hated him enough to write and mail letters explaining what a moron he was for vetoing a bill or what a villain he was for failing to nominate a certain highly capable public servant. Still, it was difficult not to read them. You got a sense of how those called "likely voters" think about political questions—not deeply, or much at all, but intensely and without distinctions. Most letter writers seemed to have ingested one or two half-understood facts that accorded with their suspicions and then worked a few inane jibes into paragraph form. They believed their own attitudes, and those of the public officials they admired, to be inerrant, and they felt free to interpret contrary views or remarks in the worst possible light. They stressed their points by putting them in dismissive, vaguely archaic phrasing. For some reason they often described the governor as "our esteemed governor": "Our esteemed governor thinks the way to help the unemployed is to do nothing." Letter writers liked to use the lawyerly "said" to indicate sarcastic disapproval: "That was before said governor got himself elected." Common expressions were often embellished by the word "proverbial": "The governor finds himself between a rock and the proverbial hard place." The phrases "need I add" and "each and every" were favorites: "Need I add that our esteemed governor has vetoed each and every bill to raise the cigarette tax?" And "so much for": "The governor says he's concerned for the disadvantaged. Yet he vetoed a bill that would have extended Medicaid to the children of low income families. So much for his credibility."

Writing surrogate letters wasn't quite so easily justified; there was something slightly but definitely dishonest about it. To get one placed, you had to sound like the real thing, but not so much that you discredited your own position or insulted the intelligence of the supporter whose name you were hoping to attach to it. You had to start the letter off with some sassy stock phrase or rhetorical question: "Representative So-and-so just doesn't get it" or "Which constitution is Senator So-and-so reading?" Then you'd make your case without sounding like you knew too much about the topic. That's where surrogate letters sometimes went wrong. They would refer to specific revenue numbers or to the names of subcommittees or explain the difference between house and senate versions of bills. Average people didn't know these things, and if a surrogate letter used them, it sounded like what it was, and editors wouldn't run them.

I spent a day writing these wretched things. It wasn't worth it unless you produced ten or fifteen; newspapers likely wouldn't print a letter taking a certain view if they got only one, but if they got a handful they'd feel bound to run one or two. It was a mind-numbing exercise: each one had to sound clumsy but not stupid; each had to approach the question from a different angle; and none could use the same vocabulary. We sent them out to the ostensible authors, and over the next two weeks or so I would see my little creations pop up in a variety of newspapers. Sometimes a few words had been changed by the surrogates, but by and large they slapped their names on the letters and forwarded them to their hometown newspapers. I felt the whole exercise was pointless, but perhaps the letters did contribute in a small way to the sense that Knotts's allegations had been grossly unfair and that the governor had acted properly. Had he? I thought so at the time, but enough time has passed that I can admit I don't know. One of the melancholy facts of political life is that your convictions tend to align with your paycheck.

The editorialists, momentarily exercised about the NGA scandal, soon forgot about it. At one point the opposition party was said to be preparing a hard-hitting advertisement excoriating the governor for improper use of state money, but it never happened. Why? Not because some independent body rendered a decision and settled the matter in the governor's favor or because the governor's public explanations were persuasive, but because it wasn't titillating enough to expand into a real scandal. I had done my little part to ensure that it blew over. I'm glad I did, really. Anything said to be an outrage by the egregious buffoon Jake Knotts deserves a full pardon. But it bothered me a little that I had done my part simply because it was my job.

6

· THE ART OF SAYING NO

The governor could sense that most of us were just bureaucrats: we weren't deeply or emotionally invested in the administration's successes or in the governor's political ambitions, but in our income and career and families; we didn't care much how history would treat him. So it was easy to put off assignments or to do them without great attention to detail. His leadership style, if that's what it was, was to counteract this tendency with erratic bouts of rage. Without notice, he would storm into the office and walk from room to room, a stack of papers in one hand, like notes for a lecture, berating the staff for laziness and incompetence. "Again," he would say, "I can't be the guy pointing this stuff out. This is your job, and your

job, and your job"—his finger pointing at various bystanders—"not mine."

The one thing consistently neglected by the staff was, as
the governor called it, the big board. This was a massive dry-
erase board in the conference room adjoining the governor's
office; its purpose was to give him an overarching view of the
administration's aims and strategies. The board was meant to
display a list of goals, various dates by which these goals were
to be accomplished, the names of legislators who were pro-
moting this or that initiative, and many other items that were
vital to know one minute and irrelevant the next. He wanted
the big board updated constantly; it should always look completely different from what it had looked like a week before.
Nat, who had excellent administrative skills, was in charge
of it.

There were two problems with the big board. The first
was that it was useless. There was such a vast array and quan-
tity of items needing to be written on it that a properly updated big board would have required its own full-time staffer.
The other problem was that the governor cared about it only
infrequently. He wouldn't bother looking at it or asking about
it for months, then suddenly it was all he could think about.
He would discern immediately that it hadn't been altered in
a month or two and collapse into a fit of angry inarticulacy.
"How am I supposed to know where I am?" he'd say, or "I'm
on the road and I'm in a black hole, and I come back here and
I look at the big board and it hasn't been updated and I'm still
in a black hole."

Sometimes Nat would spend an hour or so on the big

board when the governor was out of the office. I would sit in the conference room to keep him company; he had the look of a great artist creating a masterwork. He never seemed to have the right kinds of markers—some were the permanent kind, which wouldn't erase properly; others were out of ink—with the result that the whole thing looked like a great multicolored palimpsest. There were all sorts of categories on the big board: "the week ahead," "the long view," "don't let these die," and so on. There was one category called "the next 90 days," and under it I once noticed two items I didn't recognize. The first was "Real ID" and the second was "Shawn's Law."

———

Shawn had been killed in 2003, and now his parents wanted a law. Some people joked that when members of the General Assembly wanted badly to pass a bill, they would name it after a dead child. This wasn't fair, since some of these "dead kid laws," as they were cruelly called, were forced on legislators rather than conceived by them. Bereaved parents would ask their representative to introduce the bill—intended to prevent the means of death visited on their own unfortunate child— and since nobody wanted to be on record opposing the bill, it would make its way through committee, to first reading, back to committee, to second and third readings, to the other chamber, through first, second, and third readings, to conference, usually back to both chambers, then ratified, then to the governor, in barely any time at all. There were all sorts of dead kid laws: Rebecca's Law and Erica's Law and I don't know how many others. They were called laws even before they passed, so confident was everyone that they would.

Shawn's Law had made its way through committee to the senate floor, then to the house, then to conference in a fortnight. Shawn was a young teenager who'd been killed while driving an ATV, an all-terrain vehicle; he was the latest in a series of four or five boys who'd been killed in similar ways, and several of the state's newspapers and television news channels had run lengthy stories on this trend, as it seemed to be. Shawn's mother and father wanted a law banning kids under sixteen, I think it was, from driving ATVs while unattended by an adult.

The governor had vetoed the bill the year before and, despite some changes in this year's version, would veto it again. That decision had already been made at a "rat meeting," a ratification meeting. These were meetings of the policy staff with the governor in which staff would explain the substance of ratified bills to the governor and offer their opinions on whether he should sign the bill, veto it, or allow it to pass into law without his signature. After this, unless the right decision was plain to everyone, another member of the policy staff would take the contrary position, and the governor would listen and moderate. As a member of the press office, I wasn't required to attend rat meetings, but I liked to sit in on them if I could. It gave me a sense of what was happening, and I liked the feeling of importance it gave me to argue in favor of or against a bill that might become law for four and a half million people.

All rat meetings went more or less the same way. The first staffer would explain his or her bill and the reasons for vetoing it or not. Having been immersed in the legislation, the staffer would relay the bill's contents in a wonkish way; the governor would snap, "Come on, in English!"; and the staffer would explain it in a more decipherable way. Or, if the staffer proved incapable of explaining it to the governor's satisfaction, Stewart would mediate.

Diane, the health policy advisor, might go first. "H-three-nine-one-nine requires that out-of-state dental labs employ a dental technician registered in-state if that lab performs tech work prescribed by a dentist licensed in this state."

"Wwww," the governor would respond. "Wwwhat does that mean? Come on, guys, how many times do I have to say this? In English."

"Governor," Stewart would interject, "a lot of dentists prescribe tech work to out-of-state labs. This bill would mandate that those labs, wherever they are, employ at least one technician who's registered here, in-state."

"Okay. So, if a dentist prescribes tech work, the lab or whatever has to employ somebody registered here?"

"That's correct, sir."

Governor: "Veto. That's stupid."

Stewart: "You're clear on what the bill does?"

Governor: "Seems pretty clear. Why does some lab have to employ somebody from in-state to be valid here? That's stupid. Are there any arguments for it?"

Maybe somebody would offer an argument. Sometimes a staffer would mention that some lawmaker was really keen on getting a bill through or some other practical matter of expedience. It didn't matter who the lawmaker was or how powerful he or she was; the boss's response would be some variation on a repetitive theme: "Again, in case you haven't noticed, I don't care whether some senator likes a bill or not. This is just another stupid mandate pushed by lobbyists for their own mercenary reasons. The technicians want more business, so they hired a lobbyist to get a bill passed that forces dentists to use them instead of someone in another state. That's stupid. Veto. Next."

"Uh-hut!" That'd be Diane. Rat meetings were always punctuated by her laugh: "Uh-hut!"

Another staffer: "Next bill is S-three-four-eight. Shawn's Law. I think we're all pretty familiar with this one. Some changes from last year's bill, but basically the same idea. It would make it illegal for children under age sixteen to operate ATVs without supervision, and it would require fifteen-year-olds to pass a safety course before using them with adult accompaniment. As I say, this year's version isn't that different. My main concern here is enforcement. We'd be passing a law that—."

"Exactly." The governor grasped the point of this one without much explanation. "What are you gonna do, post DNR agents all over the state and tell 'em to watch out for kids riding ATVs? This is a joke."

"Uh-hut!"

Staffer: "There's also the issue of this safety course. It's not clear how—."

"Who's going to run that? And what are you going to

do to a kid who rides one on private property? Stop him and make him take out his safety course certificate? This is a joke. Veto."

"Uh-hut!"

———

The governor had five calendar days, excluding Sundays, to sign or veto a bill. At some point during those five days, particularly if the bill was a big deal, we might have what Nat called a fire drill. Fire drills happened when a hard deadline approached—a press conference or, as in this case, a ratification deadline—and suddenly the governor's attention became completely fixed on a single task. Maybe he and his family were going out of town that weekend and it had to be done before he left. Suddenly he'd want to discuss every conceivable argument and think through every piece of relevant data. He'd scribble on a notepad and shout questions at whoever was standing nearby. The questions usually had to do with some past veto or policy position, and generally only Stewart knew the answers.

"There was a bill in like 2004, something to do with eyesores on private property. Did we sign it or veto it?"

"I don't know" would be the answer.

"Get Stewart in here."

That person would run off to find Stewart. Then the governor would shout to the scheduling office, just outside his door, "Hey, Lewis!" Lewis would come in and the governor would ask where Stewart was. Lewis, who hadn't heard him ask for Stewart the first time, would run off to find him. This would happen four or five times in quick succession. If Stewart was at his desk or outside smoking, it wasn't a problem. If he was elsewhere, we'd see a train of young people walking through the governor's wing of the State House and in the men's room off the rotunda asking if anybody had seen Stewart. Finally Stewart would be rounded up, and he'd answer the governor's question. Then the governor would think of another question, and this one Stewart couldn't answer with the kind of precision the governor wanted (some statistic maybe) and would call into the office a policy advisor, who would be even less capable of answering it but would vow to find the answer in minutes. This would happen two or three times, and the entire office would buzz with people trying to find out how many people under seventeen had died in ATV accidents during the previous decade or how many field agents the Department of Natural Resources employed or how many states required young people to undergo ATV safety courses. And when it was over and the governor was happy with the product, one or two youngsters would still be walking around asking where Stewart was.

After the veto became known some time the next day, Shawn's parents talked to reporters outside the State House. The mother was crying.

Within a half hour the senate had reconvened and the veto had come up for a vote. A few of us went up to the gallery to watch. Almost as soon as debate started, Jakie Knotts dislodged himself from his chair and asked the president if the senator would yield.

"Senator yields," the president said.

Knotts crammed the microphone into his mouth and said, "I started out in law enforcement. I was a police offissah." He seemed to burp some of his words, as if he'd just finished a plate of barbecue and coleslaw. "And I know what it's like to go tell a parent they chil' died. I'ma tell you, it ain't fun. You tell somebody they chil' died, you seen what it does to 'em. The governor don't know what it's like to tell a parent they chil' died. I do."

The legislative staff, Jeane especially, were in disbelief. Knotts had voted to sustain the same veto the year before, and he had been heard in several private settings to pan the bill as more "feel-good legislation." His county was notoriously full of yokels, but it was adjacent to the capital city, which meant they were informed yokels, if I can put it that way, and they'd know it if their senator voted to put a lot of irksome restrictions on the use of their hunting vehicles. He'd been counted on as a sustain vote, but his hatred of the governor had evidently been too great and he was arguing to override.

"Thass the whole problem with this governor. He don't care. He don't care 'bout the people. He don't give a rat's—a rat's—behind about the people."

Debate stretched into the afternoon. The senate was about equally divided on the bill, but its supporters needed thirty-two votes to override—two thirds—and they were nowhere near that. They took turns denouncing the governor, and those who opposed the bill seemed reluctant to defend him. At last, when the clerk tabulated the final vote at a few minutes before midnight, the ayes (override) were 25, the nays (sustain) 17. The bill was dead. For the second time, the governor had successfully blocked a dead kid law, and we all prepared for the outrage-fueled press conferences and the weepy news stories and the accusatory op-eds.

A few nights later, one of the cable news channels ran a four- or five-minute segment on the governor. The Shawn's Law veto was part of the story. The reporter said, if I remember, "And he isn't afraid of saying No."

7

The presidential election was now a little less than
a year away, and the news was full of speculation
about the primaries. At that stage there were still
seven or eight candidates running in both parties' primaries;
you read and heard endless commentary about how this candidate's message was "resonating" with voters, about how that
candidate had broken fund-raising records, about how another
had switched his view on illegal immigration or cutting the
corporate income tax in order to shore up his credibility with
some constituency or other, or just with his base. You had the
feeling that these appraisals were mostly irrelevant, like some
worthless currency stockpiled in the deluded belief that its
value would soon rise. But it all seemed important at the time.

Around January a few journalists began mentioning the governor as a possible vice presidential candidate. It was always just a mention, usually, though not always, alongside other names. It was absurd to suggest vice presidential picks so long before the nominee, who would do the picking, had even been named.

A producer from one of the networks called Aaron about an interview. That a network wanted to interview the governor wasn't uncommon; in this instance, though, the subject was presidential politics. They were doing a segment on "where the party is headed," and they wanted the views of a few of the party's leaders. The governor was one. The producer told Aaron they'd be asking general questions about the direction the party would and should take over the next four years. Their camera crew would come to the State House in a week.

Over the two or three days before the interview, Nat and I worked hectically on preparing the governor. We put together a document neatly delineating possible lines of questioning, common observations made about the party and its candidates in the news media, the candidates' views, and the latest poll numbers.

We did this in the full knowledge that the governor would say he hated what we produced. When we presented it to him in his office, he looked at it for a few seconds and said, "This doesn't tell me anything."

Silence.

"Again," he said, still looking at it.

"Governor, you've barely looked at it," Nat said.

"I mean, why do I need to know"—he drew a tiny circle on one of the pages, and next to it a question mark—"why do I need to know that McCain thinks we should put tighter economic sanctions on Iran? What good's that to me?"

"It's something you should know?" Nat said in a sarcastic interrogative tone.

"There's no way they're going to ask me about Iran."

This was untrue, and I was sure the governor knew it was untrue. He didn't like to accept a document without first dismissing it as worthless. Provoking a fight with the staffers who'd written it was his way of figuring out whether or not it was what he wanted.

"Okay," Nat said, "what do you want us to find?"

Nat often tried to sidestep the governor's criticisms, which he didn't like. He wanted to cajole, reprove, instruct.

"Again," he said.

Nat and I waited.

The governor gestured at the document. "Again."

Usually at this point he said something about "digging deeper." "You've got to dig deeper," he said. "Don't just tell me stuff any college flunky could tell me."

"Like what? What would you like us to put together for you that some college flunky couldn't?"

"You tell me," the governor said.

"We should tell you?"

"Yeah." The governor looked irritated. I just sat there like a mannequin.

"We should tell you something beyond"—Nat held out his arm—"what some college flunky could tell you?"

"Yeah. Think about it."

"Actually, Governor, what we think you need to know is written right there."

"What, like McCain wants to bomb Iran?"

"Governor, why do you do this? You're being completely unreasonable."

"Okay, here's what I want. I want—."

"Wait," Nat said. "You're admitting that you're being unreasonable."

"What I want—."

"You're admitting it."

"What I want—."

"Unbelievable."

"Whatever. I want all the candidates' positions on taxes—corporate, personal, everything."

"That's in what we just gave you."

"Then I want—."

"Unbelievable."

"I want all the significant votes of every candidate on spending issues: the farm bill, the budgets, whatever appropriations bills, whatever."

He listed a few more things and they were all sensible things to ask for. Nat and I set about finding them. What was the turnout for both parties in the previous primary election? What were some significant demographic trends? How many times had the state voted for the candidate who'd gone on to win the presidency?

We worked all day on these sorts of questions. Around six or seven o'clock we brought the result to the mansion and went over the whole document with the governor in his study. He seemed agitated about the interview, scheduled for early the next morning. Nat began to fire questions at him, the sort of questions a typical DC journalist would ask: *You say such and such, Governor, but actually isn't the opposite true?* The governor enjoyed that.

I had been inside the mansion before, but never upstairs to the family's living quarters. His study was cluttered with stacks of books and piles of papers. There were pictures of his sons everywhere, and on the wall were their drawings of football players and soldiers. One of them was a strikingly lifelike representation of a soldier.

"Your boy's a good artist," I said.

The governor's face had looked tired, his eyes red, but suddenly his expression softened as he looked at the drawing. "Yeah. He's talented, isn't he?"

The interview happened at eight o'clock the following morning, evidently to the governor's satisfaction. I wasn't in the room for it; only Aaron was. He said nothing about it afterward, which meant he'd been pleased by it.

A week or so later the producer called Aaron to let him know the program would run at seven o'clock on a certain weeknight. Nat, Aaron, and I gathered around the press office's television.

Stewart came in, agitated. One of the cabinet officials, the head of the Department of Corrections, I think, had been carrying on an open feud with a senator. Stewart had been trying to adjudicate the matter, with no success. He came in cursing the senator with all his powers of invective. When he saw us gathered around the television, he asked, "What are you guys doing?"

"It's the big interview."

"Oh right, the Party Leaders of Tomorrow thing."

"Party Leaders of Today, bitch!" That was Aaron.

"Oh, I get it. It's the first round of the quadrennial Pick Me as Veep Competition."

The program started. Ten or twelve staffers were now in the room. One official after another was interviewed, in almost every case substantively. The governor of one state talked about income taxes, to which the interviewer responded aggressively. A congressman from another state talked about the dangers of political correctness and "inside the Beltway" mentalities; he too was questioned and answered skillfully. They even interviewed the mayor of some midwestern city who had interesting things to say about federal crime policy and road privatization. Then, as the voice-over mentioned something about Ronald Reagan, the camera showed our governor, sitting in his office.

"The party's looking for the next Reagan," he said. "Whether we find him remains to be seen."

And that was it. The narration went on to another subject, and the governor's face wasn't seen again. Somebody turned off the television once it became clear that that was all. Nobody said anything for a few seconds, and then Stewart began laughing, quietly at first, then loudly and uncontrollably, roaring, almost falling backward in his chair.

Nat cracked open a soda can. "Well, boys," he said, "we're looking for the next Reagan. And whether we find him—."

Stewart went silent. Aaron said, "Remains to be seen," and Stewart bellowed again.

"That was insightful," he said, his frame convulsing. "And here I was thinking we'd already found the next Reagan. But in fact that question"—he paused and looked around the room—"remains to be seen. Who knew?" He howled again, covering his mouth and saying, "We're—still—looking."

"That's it for me," Aaron said, walking out. "I'm glad you guys worked so hard on that interview."

———

Writing talking points was the most important part of my job, and the worst. Talking points are written products used for speaking engagements. They were as necessary for the governor as they are for any other politician.

Politicians are expected to speak far too much—we all feel that. David Gergen, who wrote speeches for Nixon and Ford, points out in his memoir that whereas Nixon made only a handful of public speeches in his six years as president, by the late 1990s presidents were expected to speak all the time and about everything. In 1997 alone, Gergen writes, President Clinton made 545 public speeches, more than Reagan and George H. W. Bush combined.* For the vast majority of these presidential speeches, it doesn't much matter what the president says, so long as he doesn't say anything

———

* David Gergen, *Eyewitness to Power: The Essence of Leadership, Nixon to Clinton* (New York: Simon & Schuster, 2001).

vulgar or ridiculous. The governor of course didn't speak with that kind of frequency, but there were always enough speaking engagements on his schedule to make it impossible for him to know all the requisite details about each engagement.

On a full day he might speak briefly to a group of schoolteachers from Spartanburg on the occasion of some awards ceremony, then to a group from Jasper County about a bill to raise the sales tax by 1 percent. Then two groups would come to the office for proclamation signings and photographs, one to commemorate National Career Development Month and one to mark National Square Dancing Month (the latter distinguishable by their attire). Later in the day he'd be driven to some part of the state where a corporation was announcing a $6 million expansion and the creation of 150 jobs. Then, before going home, he'd drop by the Charleston County legislative reception. The people involved in each of these events would have made the understandable but often mistaken assumption that the governor had a clear idea of who they were and what it was they were doing. That's why high-level politicians need speechwriters: not because they're so dense they need someone to tell them what to say but because no normal person can be expected to say something interesting that many times a day, on that many subjects, to that many separate groups. Talking points explain what the event is, who will be present, the event's agenda if there is one, some relevant background, and what we—the speechwriters—believe will be appropriate or interesting for the governor to say.

For the unimportant events or the ones he didn't care much about, he would wait until three or four minutes before the event began to look at the talking points. If the event was in the office or if you were with him on the road, he preferred that you tell him what the event was and what he should say.

"So what are we doing here?"

"This is the Mother of the Year Award ceremony."

"Who's getting the award?"

"Macel Dargan, from Florence."

"Why's she Mother of the Year?"

"She volunteered at McLeod Hospital for almost thirty years. She's gone on medical mission trips to Haiti and other places and taken her four children with her on many of those trips."

"How many children?"

"Four: three boys and a girl."

"What are their names?"

This is when you knew he was probing for a point of ignorance. There was no conceivable circumstance in which he would be expected to know the names of the woman's children. I would glance down at my notes and tell him the names.

"How old?"

"They're all grown."

"How long do I talk?"

The true answer to that question was *It doesn't matter. You're the governor.* He knew that to be the case, but you couldn't tell him it didn't matter how long he spoke or he'd lecture you about how everything matters. The best thing to do was to make up an answer and sound confident when you gave it. "Very short. Five minutes max."

"Okay. Wwwwwhat do I say?" Up until now he'd been looking down at the talking points or some miscellaneous papers. This was the really unpleasant part.

"I'd say—."

"Don't pause," he would say in an aggressive tone. "When I start talking, I can't pause."

Which was false. He paused all the time, and at awkward moments.

"Okay," I said.

"Don't say 'Okay,' just tell me what I'm gonna say."

"You should say—."

"Don't tell me 'You should say.' When I stand in front of those people, I can't say, 'Here's what I'm gonna say.' Just say what I'm supposed to say. Go."

"I'd say—."

"No, just say it. Go. I don't have time here."

All this happened in full view of other staffers. So I turned to them and pretended I was the speaker.

"There was an article in the *Wall Street Journal* recently," I said, putting on an absurd air of relaxed self-confidence, "about a famous musician, a pianist. A few years ago he started to practice a new piece, and as soon as he played a few bars, he thought, 'I know this piece. I've played this piece before.' But here's the weird thing: he hadn't played it before. He'd never played it in his life, or even heard it. But he had heard it before—somehow he knew it. It turns out that his mother played it over and over when she was pregnant with him."

"What's that got to do with this?"

"I mention that story," I continued, "because I think it's a powerful illustration of the influence our mothers have over our lives. Even before we come into the world—."

"Boring. Total downer. Again—you have to remember the audience. This isn't some anti-abortion group. You've got to dig deeper. Remember who you're talking to."

"Governor, I can guarantee you these people are anti-abortion."

"You don't know that."

I did know that, and so did he. "They're celebrating traditional motherhood, they're independent Baptists, and they're from Florence."

Now it would become an argument about something else. He'd get impatient and say, "Never mind, I'll think of something," and walk into the event.

It didn't matter what he said. At the Mother of the Year ceremony, middle-aged women cackled and cooed at anything the governor wanted to say. I waited outside and eavesdropped on the event.

"I read an interesting article the other day in the *Wall Street Journal*, about a musician . . ."

If the event was away from the office, and you weren't with the governor, these conversations would happen over the phone. Sometimes they were brutal. He would discover the unsatisfactory nature of the talking points four minutes before he arrived at the event. After a year or so working for him, though, these calls became so routine that they lost their sting. At four minutes before an event was to begin, you'd wait for the phone to ring. When it rang, you'd prepare to answer his questions as best you could. Maybe you had written "coat and tie" as the appropriate attire, and he'd arrive to find everyone dressed casually. Maybe you had neglected to indicate whether or not he was speaking first. It mattered: if he spoke first, what he said should be more important; if third or fourth, less so. Maybe he wanted to know some vital fact about the group he was about to address—whether they'd supported his tax plan the year before, or whether they were mostly middle-class activist types or wealthy donor types—and that fact wasn't properly denoted in the talking points.

If he called you directly, it was bad. But I got better at handling him. Once, he was about to walk into an event announcing a large investment by the Heinz Company. I'd given him four or five possibilities ("narratives," he called them), but he hated them all. "Tell me something interesting!" He was almost shouting into the phone, but I couldn't think of anything else to say about the making of ketchup. Then, as if by inspiration, I remembered a joke I used to tell in school. "Okay," I said, "how about this. A few statistics for you. Did you know that, according to two major studies conducted at Yale and Oxford Universities, over half of all cases of heart disease could have been prevented by the simple expedient of consuming one tomato a week?"

"That's not true," he said. "You've got that wrong. But go on."

"Did you know, furthermore, that a modest increase in one's consumption of tomato phosphate, an ingredient found in Heinz ketchup and steak sauce, can cut your risk of colon cancer by sixty percent?"

"That's stupid," he said. "Where are you getting this?"

"And did you know, finally, that approximately ninety-one percent of statistics are made up on the spot?"

There was a long pause. "That's good. I like that."

"It should get some laughs," I said. "By the way, I made up 'tomato phosphate.' I don't even know what that is." But he had hung up.

———

That summer the governor became even more cantankerous about talking points than he was ordinarily. That was the summer when veep speculation was at its not very considerable height. Reporters from national media would show up at otherwise insignificant events to file reports on one of the politicians on everybody's list of attractive running mates.

Aaron had gotten a call from a reporter with one of the national papers saying he'd be at an event the following week, a groundbreaking for a new police academy, where the governor was to speak for five minutes or so. A few legislators would be there too but probably few if any local media; usually it wasn't something the governor would fret over, except in the routine sense of claiming he disliked what I'd written and having me redraft the talk an hour or so before he left for the event. Two or three days earlier he was already telling me, "We're not there yet," which meant I had to rewrite everything.

These were hard times. Rick, the chief of staff, had left in order to run for the state senate. Stewart had been made chief of staff, and Nat had been moved to Stewart's office as head of cabinet affairs and operations. Mack, whom I'd always suspected of possessing a keener intelligence than his tobacco chewing suggested, had left to become an academic. We had hired another speechwriter, Chris, but he wasn't useful yet, and for a few weeks I was the only one writing anything.

There were two things the governor wanted at events like this. One was to mention Rosa Parks. For him, Rosa Parks sitting on a seat in the white section of a Montgomery bus encapsulated a beautiful political ideal: changing everything, stopping everything, bringing a whole society to its knees, just by saying No. But he couldn't mention Rosa Parks on most occasions; it just didn't work. I once tried to suggest other historical figures who did similar sorts of things—Lech Walesa, Martin Luther—but he didn't think they had the same appeal for the kind of people he usually addressed, which I'm sure was true.

The other thing he liked—and this applied to every talk— was to say something interesting and relevant that nobody was expecting. He hated the thought of being the politician who says the same predictable boring things at every event; he wanted to walk into every speaking engagement armed with a story or fact or witty remark that would make him stand out in the minds of those who heard him. But he would not trust me, or anybody, to discern what was an appropriate remark for the occasion. It had to "feel right" to him, which it only rarely did.

He liked stories, especially stories drawn from history. And only stories involving people whose names everyone had heard of. All foreign names (Lech Walesa) were out. And generally only American stories, unless they were stories about governments bankrupting themselves, of which there were not many. He also liked the story of William Wilberforce, the English reformer and parliamentarian who was largely responsible for Britain abolishing the slave trade.

For the police academy's groundbreaking I had prepared five narratives. I walked into his office. I didn't see him. "Sir?"

"Yeah," I heard him groan.

On the other side of the room, behind some chairs, he was on his back, resting on a giant yellow ball. I'd heard he had back trouble. He looked at me sideways. "It's called an exercise ball. My sister gave it to me."

"Right. Ah, your talk at the police academy."

"What d'you got?" he asked, without getting up, shifting from side to side on the ball. "Let's hear the talk. Go."

By this time I was used to being told to "give the talk" to him, though the horizontal posture made it slightly awkward.

"Not far from here is Maxcy Gregg Park," I began. "I wonder how many of you know who General Maxcy Gregg was. At Sharpsburg, in September Eighteen-sixty-two, General Gregg's brigade was confronted by a brigade of untrained Connecticut volunteers who had loaded their rifles for the first time two days before the battle. Gregg's men had been through several battles already. They'd been together from the beginning of the war. The result—."

"Next," he said from the exercise ball.

I stared at him. "The result—."

"Next."

"General Gregg's—."

"Next."

Then I said as fast as I could, "General-Gregg's-men-slaughtered-the-Connecticut-men-by-a-ratio-of-nine-to-one."

"What's that supposed to prove?"

"The value of training. The Connecticut men hadn't trained. Gregg's men were well-trained. Most of them had been at Shiloh. This is a police academy. Where they train. Train people. To do police stuff. If you don't train, you won't do it well. Message: Training is important."

"Next."

I went straight to the next theme without arguing. "Winston Churchill spent the years leading up to the Second World War advocating—."

"Next."

"Are you serious? You didn't—."

"Next. C'mon, next."

"The Olympic downhill skier—."

"Next," he said, still lying on the yellow ball. "These people don't care about downhill skiing."

"It's funny, though. This downhill skier fell at the Olympics like twenty feet out of the box."

"That's not funny. It's tragic. Next."

"James Madison—."

"Next."

"I wonder if anyone knows who created the first police

force?" I waited for the "Next," but it didn't come, so I kept going. "It was Robert Peel, prime minister of—."

"Next."

I stared at him. "I'm fresh out."

Slowly he pulled himself up off the exercise ball. "You're not saying anything interesting."

Ten minutes later I would think of several sizzling replies, but I wouldn't have had the courage to say any of them to his face. At the moment I just stared at him like an idiot. At last I asked, "What sort of thing are you looking for here?"

"Something magical. Something no one's thought of. Wwwww—whatever. Just something that'll make people say, 'Oh, I never thought of that.' Not something about Wwwww—William Peel or whoever."

I went back to the press office and worked for another two hours, then came to him with four or five more ideas, but nothing worked. At last I asked Nat to help me come up with something. What I really wanted was for Nat to go into the governor's office with me when I pitched my ideas. When the governor got into one of his unreasonable moods, he would object to anything for any reason—a misplaced comma, the word "gallant"—and use it as an excuse to throw people out of the office and demand a complete do-over or redraft. Nat had a way of talking to the governor at these times that kept him from interrupting. He would start talking rapidly, as if possessed, and even if what he was saying didn't make sense, the governor wouldn't stop him. Nat would keep talking until the governor heard something he couldn't object to. This was a talent I did not have and could not cultivate. I have to think hard before I say anything. Aaron had a talent for talking creatively, and of course Stewart had it. But Aaron and Stewart tended to fall back too readily on stock phrasing. Nat had a way of talking fast and creatively and giving his words an aura of excitement and logical cohesion they wouldn't possess if you saw them written on paper. He would suddenly say, "What if—what if—what if we—what if you said—," and you couldn't help assuming that whatever came next was probably worth listening to.

So I asked Nat if he'd come with me when I suggested a few narratives. He agreed. I wrote for an hour or so, showed Nat what I'd come up with, and we both walked into the governor's office.

"Wwwww," the governor said, looking up from a notepad with a blank stare. "Okay. Go."

I wanted to start with James Madison and the War of 1812 and how America learned from its mistakes, so this time I just left out Madison's name. "After the Revolution, many Americans were starting to conclude that the Atlantic Ocean made the new nation more or less impervious to attack."

Instantly I knew I'd blundered.

"'Impervious?'" the governor repeated, staring at me with a deadpan look. "'Impervious to attack?'"

"Governor," I said, "you don't have to use these words, obviously. We're just talking about the stories, the—."

"No, but this is a serious point," he said. "'Impervious to attack.' You don't sound like you know who you're talking to. I hate that."

"The point is—."

"I know what the point is. But you're not—thinking—about—the audience." Now he was pounding his desk. "You've got—to think—about—the audience. These are regular guys at this thing, law enforcement types, not a bunch of academics who go around talking about things being 'impervious to attack.'"

"I understand that—."

"You don't understand. It's obvious you don't get it." He leaned back in his chair, stared at the ceiling, and said, slowly, "What would the—the—the truck driver—what would the trucker at the—the—the feed-and-seed think of it? You've got to think about the truck driver at the feed-and-seed."

Nat, who'd been pretending to write things down on a scrap of paper, said, "Why would a truck driver be in a feed-and-seed?"

The governor stared at him. "No, the point—."

"Seriously," Nat said, "does this truck driver have some kind of side interest in farming?"

"Okay, I got it," the governor said, "you got me."

"Governor, Barton has a good story here. Just ignore the issue of phrasing for a minute and hear him out."

From there I went on to tell the governor about the War of 1812 and how the young nation had learned the importance of maintaining a standing professional army and how it couldn't rely on a bunch of farmers to come together in times of crisis and form a lethal fighting force to repel a well-trained invader. At last he settled on something, I don't remember what. Maybe it was 1812 or maybe some other idea, or maybe it was one of his usual bits of rigmarole; he was very fond of a quote from some historical novel, something about land being more than dirt, although he would tell it as if it weren't fiction but history. Anyhow he settled on something and left.

It must have been seven or eight o'clock by then, and my wife had been calling, leaving messages asking when I'd be home. I hadn't called her back. These were bad days for us. I was ignoring her, fixated instead on pleasing a man who could not be pleased. I didn't work the long hours some of my colleagues did—Stewart never left the State House, as far as I knew—but even when I went home I'd find myself fretting over op-eds and agitatedly telling the children not to talk to me while I took a call from the governor or Aaron about the next day's talking points. Laura would ask, with some logic, why I was getting so worked up over an op-ed or a speech when I knew he would ignore it or find a reason to dismiss it. I didn't have an answer. I was either worrying over work or reading books; my income couldn't support a family of five (we'd had a third daughter by then), and I had to turn out book reviews and essays as fast as I could. My colleagues would see me eating lunch over a biography of Hardy or a book about Scottish literature, and they would assume I was learned. In fact I was just surviving, barely.

Between work and writing my mind was almost completely elsewhere. Unlike other men my age who ignore their families, though, I couldn't point to a hefty income to justify my absenteeism. Laura dealt with it, but sometimes we shouted at each other. Sometimes fights would arise about my work, but usually the cause was something else entirely, and I wouldn't know how it started or how to solve it.

That night I didn't go immediately home. I walked out the west wing door intending to meet some friends a few blocks from the State House for a drink. But instead of walking to the bar, I just stood there, looking at the sky. A breeze made the sweat on my back feel cool. I leaned against the wall. Just above my head was a bronze star marking the spot where one of Sherman's cannonballs had struck the building, ripping away a chunk of stone.

Stewart came out to smoke. "You have fun with the—what was it—the police academy groundbreaking?"

"Yeah."

He lit a cigarette.

"You want to kill him, don't you?" he asked after a minute or two.

"Do you?"

"I've wanted to kill him many times," he said in a calm, almost soporific voice. "He's a terrible person."

"Is he? I mean, you really think he's a terrible person?"

"In a way, yeah. You can't get to where he is without being a terrible person. At this level, they're all self-aggrandizing bastards. You should go with us to NGA next time. Watch these guys and their staff. Petty, mean-spirited, vicious little tramps who would step on anyone if it made them look good in front of their boss. Now I grant you, some are better at hiding it than our boss, but in their dark little hearts they're all just as bad as he is."

We stood watching the sun go down for two or three minutes. Through the trees it looked as if it were just above the river. Union troops had crossed that river many years before.

"Just think," he said, the breeze driving the smoke sideways from his mouth. "If you can do this, you can do anything."

"I keep hearing that."

I wondered if that was just a platitude, or if it was true.

8

From January to May, when the legislature did the bulk of its business, the governor would do a press event every fortnight or so, sometimes more often. Some of these were bill signings, but most happened just before the legislature did something he considered foolish. He would urge the legislators not to go through with it, they'd go through with it, and our office would put out a scathing press release or a scathing media statement or, if the governor felt strong enough about it, a scathing op-ed. We did a lot of scathing.

Most press events were boring, highly predictable. The governor could sense this, and sometimes he would do crazy things to compensate reporters for the boredom. Once, just as

a press conference outside a gas station was about to begin—
the governor was denouncing a hike in the cigarette tax—he
decided to move the whole thing inside. It was a preposterous thing to do: outside there was a lovely backdrop of gas
pumps and a giant advertisement for cigarettes. Inside he had
to stand in a narrow aisle crammed with candy bars and po-
tato chips. One reporter had to ask questions from the next
aisle, over a display of soft drinks. When the stories appeared
the next day, the governor's head appeared just in front of a
fluorescent poster declaring "3 MUSKETEERS 12-PACK
ONLY $4.99." There was always the threat of such weirdness
at one of our press conferences. Maybe reporters liked that.
They always seemed to show up, even if we told them almost
nothing of what it was to be about.

It was the spring of 2008, and we had information the
revelation of which interested state as well as national media.
After 9/11 the U.S. Congress had passed a law requiring states
to alter their driver's licenses to meet national criteria, in effect creating a national ID card, called Real ID. If a state did
not comply by the deadline, its governor could apply for an
extension, which (federal authorities implied) would be readily granted. Failure either to comply or to apply for an extension, however, would result in citizens of that state no longer
being admitted to federal buildings or on airplanes that flew
through federal airspace.

This was perfect material for the governor to mount a re-
bellion. He was never interested in Southernness or the Lost
Cause, but he relished the idea of spurning federal authority.
An attempt by federal bureaucrats to force states to revamp

their driver's licenses, then to make the states pay for it, all for the purpose of compiling a centralized database of personal identities: it seemed calculated to ignite his imagination. Best of all was the fact that the feds, in their communications with our office, didn't stress the consequences of noncompliance, leading us to believe they wouldn't actually do anything about it if we refused to comply.

If you worked for the governor for any length of time, even if you just knew a little about him, you knew he would refuse to apply for an extension of the Real ID deadline. Doing so would have compromised his brand. He wouldn't be criticized for complying with the law, except by libertarians. But if he complied, it would bother his conscience and, more important, he would look like any other politician.

Of course we waited until the day of the deadline to make the announcement. Aaron put off reporters with the usual verbiage about how "we're studying all the implications of the law" and "we'll come to a conclusion shortly."

A week beforehand the smarter editorialists, the ones who already knew what the governor would do without waiting for a press conference announcing the decision, began to describe apocalyptic visions. They spoke of contingencies under the pretense that they could influence the decision: "If he refuses to ask Washington for an extension, the citizens of this state will suffer the consequences of his arrogance," and so on.

About six months before this, the General Assembly had passed, with overwhelming majorities, a binding resolution refusing to comply with Real ID. That was when very few of the legislators knew what it was and it was generally thought that neither Congress nor Homeland Security was serious about it. Federal initiatives like this get started all the time, but then they peter out, either because administrations change or because they're discovered to be unenforceable or too expensive. Or they're enforced and no one notices. Now that Homeland Security clearly intended to keep Real ID alive, legislators who'd voted for the resolution began pretending they hadn't or explaining that they didn't realize the feds, whom they continued to denounce, would keep us from boarding airplanes.

The press conference, in which we would release copies of a letter from the governor to the secretary of Homeland Security announcing that the state would not apply for an extension on compliance, was to take place in the rotunda of the State House. People began arriving about an hour beforehand, not journalists but the public as well. Some of them wore Confederate flag lapel pins. Some of them had dreadlocks and nose rings and enormous backpacks, as if they'd hiked from somewhere far away. There were families whose children carried Bibles, and there were four or five gay activists (or so I took them to be) carrying rainbow flags. Some of them brought signs saying "No Big Brother" and "Down with Fed ID" and "Don't Take the Chip." A black man held up a sign saying "Screw the Feds"; one lady with long hair in a French braid carried a sign saying "Real ID = Mark of the Beast." She was standing right beside the podium. Nat, who had an eye for these things, told another staffer to pretend to be a security handler and ask people if they wouldn't mind stepping away from the podium.

At last the governor began the long walk from the end of the State House's west wing to the podium at the center of the rotunda. Cameras flashed, and some of the rowdier onlookers shouted, "Give us some good news, Governor" and "Stand up to the bastards." He approached the podium, cameras flashing even more rapidly. There was no one behind him.

"Aahh," he began.

"Give us some hope, Governor!"

Everybody laughed.

"Aahh," he said again. "Ah, the purpose of this press availability is to announce this administration's intention"—a brief pause—"not to file for an extension with regard to Real ID."

Cheers erupted from the onlookers. The governor maintained an expression of gravity, but you could see he loved it.

He began again, and a man in a giant cowboy hat and a black leather jacket shouted, "Yeah, Gov, yeah!"

Everybody laughed, even the reporters. The governor smiled a little.

"Aaaahh."

He went on to enumerate the six or eight reasons why we would not comply with this "costly, unfunded, and dangerous mandate." Nobody looked bored. The print reporters scribbled on their pads for a full ten minutes. The onlookers nodded and said, "Yesssss." When the governor stopped talking there were questions, some from the onlookers, which wasn't orthodox but he answered them. The reporters went on scribbling.

The reporter Donald Hatfield asked, "Governor, if the people who put you into office aren't allowed to board passenger airplanes because their license isn't recognized by the federal government, are you willing to accept responsibility for that?"

"I don't think it'll come to that, Donald," the governor said. "But I'd just say three things." Saying there were three things was the governor's way of giving himself a second or two to think about the answer; sometimes there were two things, sometimes just one.

"First," he said, "the question was whether I was prepared to go along with a $14 billion unfunded mandate so that the federal government can impose a centralized national ID system. I'm not prepared to saddle this state's taxpayers with that kind of burden for something they didn't ask for and, I believe, don't want."

The onlookers cheered again.

The governor looked around to take another question.

"You said there were three things, sir," Hatfield said. "What was the second?"

"Right, no. Yes."

We waited.

"Wwww," he said. "I mean—."

Hatfield: "The first was about an unfunded mandate. And the second—."

Nat mumbled to me, "Hatfield's such a jackass."

"Right. Second, I was just going to point out that the legislature passed a law a few months ago saying we would not participate in the federal Real ID mandate. I had an obligation to uphold state law. It's as simple as that."

Hatfield didn't ask for the third point. After the questions, eight or ten reporters surrounded the governor. The cameras, some of them from national media, wanted face time with him.

Thus began a year when, despite the governor's weirdness and the vehemence with which he was hated by the legislature, you had the feeling that he was out in front. Working for the governor wasn't something anyone would look back on with fondness or regret that it ended. Many days were intolerable. But around this time you could at least take pleasure in the fact that you worked for a man with courage and imagination.

A few days later the secretary of Homeland Security replied to the governor's letter. He acknowledged the governor's position, regretted it, but made no reference to consequences.

9

The governor now trusted me to write his letters. I wrote a good many personal letters for him, most of them responses to letters from acquaintances or allies or critics, but some of them self-generated. With a little help from my list of his favorite words and phrases, his incommodious style now came to me naturally. Once he even told me that I had "cracked the code." He meant it as a compliment, but I sometimes feared the habits would become unshakable; one day I'd start work on a book review and find myself writing "I'd simply say three things" or "It speaks to this larger notion of where do we go from here."

The governor received hundreds of letters every week. Many of these were written by people who were angry at him for some reason; others were requests for parole and pardon or for help in some appalling domestic situation. The Correspondence Office had ways of responding to all of these. But there were always a few letters Correspondence didn't know what to do with. Those fell to me. There were lots of invitations to weddings and oyster roasts and block parties. I would regret those, always in the governor's voice. But there were odd ones too. Somebody would write to ask his advice on getting into politics. Another would ask what he was doing about recycling, or why he didn't wear a wedding ring, or whether he thought the state of Israel had a right to exist. A great many letters asked how the governor would define the American Dream; some of these were from children and had probably been school assignments, but some of them seemed to be from ordinary people who just wanted to know, which was touching in a way. I developed an arsenal of responses to these and other questions. I had an "American Dream" response, a "How do I get into politics?" response, a "Won't you please run for president?" response, and many others. The trick was to use the maximum number of words with the maximum number of legitimate interpretations. Put that way, it sounds terrible, but there's no other way to do it. If a constituent writes to ask the governor the best way to get into politics, and you (in the governor's voice) write back using words like "I think you should run" or "Go for it," you may soon hear about some nitwit running for county council claiming he's been endorsed by the governor. Or take the "Won't you please run for president?" letters, of which there were many around this time. In case the letter was made public, you couldn't have the governor responding in a way that could be construed as an admission of an intent to run or of an interest in running, or as an admission of anything. At the same time, though, you wouldn't want to deny an intention to run for president because that would have been obviously dishonest and, as I thought, soon disprovable. In both these cases you'd want to give the letter writers at least two full paragraphs in response; otherwise it looked cold and dismissive. So you would elongate every sentence with superfluous phrases. "I believe" would become "I have every reason to believe," and platitudinous observations would be prefaced by "What I'd say—and I am absolutely certain about this—is that . . ." The phrase "going forward" was very useful, as was "from where I stand."

The governor once received a request for a letter congratulating a young man for gaining acceptance to a venerable boys' choir. What you'd want to say was "That's a remarkable honor for you, and I wish you the best of luck as you sharpen your talent." But you needed more verbiage to fill out the paragraph, so you'd write, "That's an incredible honor for you, and I do wish you the best of luck as you sharpen the remarkable talent you so obviously possess in spades." (The governor was always saying people had qualities "in spades," and he liked to make sentences trail off into superfluous phrases.) One sentence gives you only six or seven extra words, but if you do this for five or six sentences in succession, you've turned a perfunctory note into a heartfelt letter on which some time was spent.

Everybody complains that politics separates words from their meanings, and this is part of the reason why. Words are useful, but often their meanings are not. Sometimes what you want is feeling rather than meaning, warmth rather than content. And that takes verbiage. The trick for me was to use the governor's verbiage rather than the formulaic balderdash of contemporary politics. I faced the temptation every day. I'd find myself writing "kicking the can down the road" or "ushering in a new era of fiscal responsibility" and I'd quickly tap the delete key, feeling slightly ashamed. Sometimes, though, I just couldn't avoid it. It fell to me to write the governor's official letter celebrating Emergency Medical Services Awareness Week, to be read at an annual gathering of ambulance drivers, lifeguards, and so on. I wondered what he could say to these people that wouldn't sound totally thoughtless, but nothing came to mind. They weren't soldiers, or even police officers, so that body of rhetoric (honor, duty, country) was mostly unavailable. I started to explain my dilemma to Nat. "So here's a question," I said. "Do Emergency Medical Services personnel—."

"Lay their lives on the line every day?" he said, without looking up. "Absolutely."

That winter remains in my mind as one great blizzard of verbiage. It started with the insolvency of the Employment and Workforce Commission. The Commission had been running through funds budgeted for unemployment benefits at an alarming rate, and nobody had noticed that it was about to run out completely. The Commission blamed the legislature, the legislature blamed the Commission, and the governor blamed the legislature and the Commission, but especially the Commission.

The Commission, it turned out, would have to apply for

federal money to avoid a shortfall, and for the application to be legal the governor would have to sign it. It was a perfect set-up for him. He refused to sign the application unless the Commission agreed to his demands, one of which was an independent audit. The Commission delayed. The deadline approached; if it were to pass, the Commission would be unable to issue unemployment checks.

There was great outrage from the people known for great outrage. Everybody (well, everybody in the state's media—but it felt like everybody everywhere) was talking about "playing chicken." The governor was "playing chicken" with the Employment and Workforce Commission; there was a "game of chicken" going on between the state's chief executive and its workforce agency. The governor was also said to be "holding the unemployed hostage" in his vainglorious attempt to get what he wanted from a government agency; sometimes he was said to be "holding the unemployed hostage to his libertarian ideology" or "holding a state agency hostage for political gain." *The State* actually combined these two images in one of its editorials: "You do not play chicken with the lives of 77,000 laid-off citizens, holding them hostage for your own political purposes." No, I supposed, you do not.

He wouldn't give in. Outraged op-eds and letters to the editor proliferated, all about hostage-taking and chicken-playing. As the apocalypse approached, it became pretty clear that the commissioners were on the defensive; all they had to do was agree to an audit, but for some reason they wouldn't. The governor did a series of interviews explaining his position. In each one he said that the Commission hadn't reformed itself despite the fact that abuses of the unemployment benefits system had become notorious all over the state. People were calling our office all the time to tell us about abuses. Someone told Aaron about a guy who'd been fired for urinating in his employer's meat locker but who had nonetheless been eligible for unemployment benefits. The governor liked that one. In the interviews he would almost always mention a guy who'd "urinated in a meat locker." At first I wondered about the wisdom of this—I would wince each time he said it—but it seemed effective. The line was instanced in many an editorial, and soon that puddle of pee joined the chickens and the hostages.

There was a good deal of panic too among the public. People drawing unemployment benefits were led to believe those checks would stop coming, although it seems to me there was never much chance of that happening. The governor sensed, correctly, that the commissioners weren't going to take the fight all the way; they were in it for their six-figure salaries for doing nothing, the expenses-paid trips, the important-looking license tags; they had no interest in getting blamed for poor people going without their unemployment pittance. They were sufficiently intelligent to envision the nightly television reports of single mothers crying because they had nowhere else to turn and laid-off store clerks and mechanics saying they were trying to find work but it wasn't easy. The commissioners knew the governor wouldn't get all the blame.

The panic was real. Any time there was a story about it in the news, especially on television news, the phones would start ringing and not let up for forty-five minutes to an hour.

Bridget, the receptionist, would transfer most of them to Constituent Services. But often all the lines were busy and she would talk callers through their problems herself. Bridget was a small, roundish woman, black, with a giant marked-up King James Bible always open on her desk. She loved to talk about personal crises, her own or the other person's, it didn't matter, and walking past the front desk you'd sometimes hear her telling a caller, "Jesus is gon' bring you through this." "Honey," she'd be saying, "He knows about your problems. He knows, and He cares. And honey, He don't make no mistakes. He gon' bring you through. Have you ever made it through something you didn't think you was gon' make it through? Was He there the whole time, did He bring you through? M-hm. Thass right. He did. And He will again, honey. You got to believe that. You remember Joseph? Did Gott leave Joseph in that dungeon? No He ditt not, no He ditt not. He brought him out, He brought him *up* is what He did. Put him second in command under Pharaoh. And He gon' bring you through this too, baby."

Bridget didn't get a great deal of respect from our office; mostly, it was felt, she just sat in that chair and talked on the phone. But many of the callers she spoke to were agitated, people who called because they blamed the governor for whatever worried them. By the time they hung up, things were going to be all right. I suspect Bridget was one of the governor's most effective political assets.

Just before the deadline, the Commission submitted to an outside audit, the governor signed for the federal loans, and the unemployment checks kept coming.

Calls kept coming too, but this time they were supportive. Constituent Services kept a tally. Before the Commission caved, the calls ran 4 or 5 to 1 against us; afterward they ran 4 or 5 to 1 in our favor. I don't remember if there was a final tally, but that's the way it usually was with constituent reaction. Angry people came before; admirers came after. It happened that way again the following summer, only this time the stakes were much higher.

10

Around this time the word "stimulus" became part of every working day. The new president was pushing Congress to pass what the news media liked to call a "stimulus package," a giant spending measure designed to "jump-start" or "stimulate" or "revive" an economy that, according to the metaphor, was moribund. The size of this package kept growing; reports cited $400 billion, then $500 billion, then $675 billion, and nowhere, so far as I could tell, was there any explanation of what was responsible for this growth. I remember this clearly because, although I've never understood numbers at all, I was used to thinking about our little state's $5 billion General Fund and $19 billion total budget. These were the big numbers to me. And now Congress was debating a single bill—not the budget itself, but just an ordinary piece of legislation—that was twenty, twenty-five, thirty-five times larger than the state's entire budget. For the first time in my life I considered the fact that a billion is a thousand millions.

The governor was in demand. Almost every day, it seemed, we were preparing talking points for another television interview. He was one of only a few politicians in the country who could talk knowledgeably about fiscal policy in broad terms, and he was the sort of person who, in contrast to most of his peers, might say something interesting at any moment. As maladroit as he usually was with words, occasionally he'd find some phrase that expressed the forebodings of millions. In one interview with one of the cable networks, he worried that the United States was creating a "savior-based economy," an economy in which "what matters is not how good your product is to the consumer but what your political connection is to those in power." Instantly the phrase was everywhere, and I wished I could take credit for it.

It was often said during these years that the relationship between the governor and the legislature was as sour as it had been in generations. I don't know if that was true in any verifiable sense; I doubt it. But now, in the winter and spring of his greatest and worst year, it certainly felt true. Legislators sensed that his attention was elsewhere; they knew what his ambitions were, and many of them longed to show the world that he wasn't the brave and winsome statesman many people thought they saw. He was popular, and they hated him. For the most part, though, they couldn't come up with any way to discredit him, unless you count overriding nearly all his vetoes.

Occasionally they'd come out with some gimmicky ploy, but it all remained pretty silly. In March, for example, Senator Leatherman and Speaker Harrell, together with the newly appointed state university president, staged a press conference showcasing a new jobs plan. This consisted, strangely, of a pyramid: on the lower parts of the pyramid were written the names of various state agencies; in the middle were the names of other state agencies; and at the top were the words "Economic Development Executive Council." It wasn't absolutely clear how such a thing would result in greater employment opportunities for actual people, but the purpose of the jobs plan wasn't to carry it out, since it had already been carried out and was nothing but a confusing, top-heavy bureaucratic bungle; the purpose rather was to show how concerned Leatherman and Harrell were about the economic well-being of the state. Unlike the governor.

Nat and I were at the press conference. You couldn't hear most of what was said because they'd made the unfortunate choice of staging it near a busy road. The reporters seemed perplexed about what the pyramid meant. One of them called it a "triangle."

I'm sure Leatherman's and Harrell's staffers told their bosses that the press conference was a huge success, that it was all over the media, that they were creating a "narrative" about how the governor cared more about his national ambitions than about jobs in his own state. But it was a petty shot, and you could tell journalists weren't buying it. They were prepared to accept the allegation that the governor had his eye on Washington but not that the legislature's leadership, with their preposterous pyramid, had something new or better to offer.

During February and March the governor became his party's most salient critic of the new president's economic stimulus, which Congress passed in mid-February. Every other day, it seemed, he was on cable TV news or talk radio or speaking on the phone to a *Washington Post* or *New York Times* reporter. Often he'd be introduced as "one of the president's most outspoken critics." And he was traveling more. Any governor, certainly any popular one, speaks from time to time at out-of-state events, either to do favors for other politicians or to make connections with potential high-level donors (or, sometimes, just because it's fun). But in these months the governor was flying everywhere all the time—to Austin, to Jackson, to Chicago, to Anaheim.

He didn't speak exclusively on the stimulus bill at all these engagements, but the topic of that bill, and of government spending generally, was never far away at any of them. Why was he so deeply opposed to it? The idea behind the stimulus was to pump large amounts of cash into the economy in order to ignite consumer spending and, in turn, growth. The governor thought that idea was foolish for many reasons, but the two that led him to oppose the policy with all his energy were these: the cash was borrowed, and most of it would pass from the federal government to state governments. He understood the culture and habits of government well enough to know that that federal money wouldn't be used to spur economic growth but to balance state budgets. Maybe it was a good idea to help states shore up their budgets and maybe it wasn't, but that wasn't the justification given for the stimulus, and in any case it would have no effect on economic growth. And he understood that, when the stimulus failed to achieve its purpose, people would remember that it was he who had inveighed against it with greater fervor than anybody else.

All this was happening while the legislature was in session, so the workload in our office became almost intolerable. I was doing all my usual duties: writing remarks for grand openings and graduation ceremonies and responding to every well-wisher who wrote a letter to the governor asking whether he liked barbecue or if he had any thoughts on energy efficiency or whether he would sign a photograph for a nephew or grandson. Now I was also drafting op-eds on the inchoate "bailout culture" of Washington, DC, writing talking points for televised interviews, collecting articles from the *Wall Street Journal*, *Washington Post*, and *New York Times* on debates over monetary policy, and responding to every swooning enthusiast or angry crank who wrote letters telling the governor to "stand firm" against the stimulus or to stop "playing politics" during a national emergency.

The governor himself was constantly agitated. Ordinarily he would dislike my drafts, but he would at least use what I'd written to create his own versions. Now he either hated what I'd written or bypassed me altogether. He would explode into the press office, hair disheveled, wearing jeans and a tattered T-shirt, and want to know some fact about hyperinflation in Zimbabwe or interwar Germany or Argentina during the 1980s. Once you gave him an answer, he'd disappear into his office again, and eventually he'd give Aaron the finished product and tell him to pitch it to one of the national papers. Some of these were printed, but many were not. One that wasn't contained the sentence "Oddly enough, the silver lining to graying economic and financial clouds may well be that reforms that have previously fallen on deaf ears may be a little bit more politically palatable."

Sometimes he'd forget which products had been drafted for him and which he'd written himself. Once, he came into the conference room and held up a piece of paper. Stewart, Paul, Gil, and I were in the room. "Who wrote this?" he asked. "It doesn't have a name on it. Again, always put a name on it." Rather than telling us what it was, the governor had us all look at it. It was a draft of a veto letter. I hadn't written it. Paul said he hadn't.

"Oh, that was mine," Gil said. "Sorry. Forgot to put my name."

"Okay," the governor said in an unpleasant tone. "What's this?" He then read aloud a dreadful sentence. We all sat in silence. He looked at Gil. "I'm asking," he said. "What is this?"

Gil, whose involuntary response to tense situations was to giggle, made a staccato sound with his throat and said, "I'm a terrible writer."

"No!" the governor almost shouted. "It doesn't have anything to do with whether you're a good writer or not. You don't have to be a good writer to know that that sentence"— he slapped the paper and, in his rage, didn't know what to call the sentence. Finally he said, "Represents a poor effort."

Then he did something that surprised even Stewart. He held up the offending paper and, slowly, ripped it from top to bottom. He then dropped the pieces into a trash can and walked out.

Gil held back tears.

What it had taken me two years to realize, and what I suspect Gil never learned, is that the governor wasn't trying to hurt you. For him to try to hurt you would have required him to acknowledge your significance. If you were on his staff, he had no knowledge of your personhood. In such an instance as this, he was giving vent to his own anxieties, whatever they were. It was as if you were one of those pieces of cork placed in the mouths of wounded soldiers during an amputation. The soldier didn't chew the cork because he hated it but because it was therapeutic to bite hard. Often I felt like that piece of cork. For weeks at a time I would drive to work in the morning nervous to the point of vomiting. I wasn't worried about any one thing—it was everything. Almost every day threatened to produce some new debacle: an oversight or blunder that would provoke the governor to wonder with inarticulate rage how someone could do such a moronic thing. I would find myself longing for a job as a liquor store cashier or a mailman or a pizza delivery guy, some inconspicuous functionary who had no connection with allegedly important things and allegedly important people. I remember there was a middle-aged man who worked for the State House maintenance crew; one of his duties, or maybe his only duty, was to make sure the building's lightbulbs still worked. I would see him wandering around the State House looking up at the various light fixtures. Sometimes I'd see him at the top of a ladder changing a bulb. He would come into the press office, look up at the lights and, satisfied that all were working, walk out. He always wore a tattered New York Mets baseball cap. He didn't seem anxious. I wanted to be him.

The governor made the decision early to do everything he could to stop that federal money from transferring to the state. He had criticized the bill in innumerable television interviews and op-eds. When it passed Congress in February, he had the choice of dropping the issue and taking the money on the grounds that what was done was done. Lots of people, mainly those who didn't know much about either him or politics, thought that's what he would do. At some point, though, maybe in an op-ed or an interview, it became clear that he intended to refuse the money.

There were lots of persuasive piecemeal arguments for turning it down. It would be two or three years before that much money could pass through the various stages of government and be injected into the economy, if it ever reached the private sector at all. But of course it wouldn't; the supposedly stimulatory funds would be eaten away by bureaucratic processing and so do nothing to stimulate anything but the public sector. Accepting several billion dollars in nonrecurring funds would mean losing that very large source of income two years later when the money ran out; then what? And there were the notorious strings attached to the funding; the federal government never gives states money without telling them how it must and must not be used, and the stimulus bill itself required that, in order to get large portions of the money, states first had to expand Medicaid and unemployment eligibility to levels that, once the stimulus funds dried up, would be unsustainable. You can see how boring all these arguments were. They're good, in a desiccated logical sense, but they're boring. For the average person they don't amount to much compared with this message: The money's going to be spent anyway; we're paying for it; why in the land of the living wouldn't we take it?

The governor had no gift for articulating complex arguments, and when he put forward his views on the unwisdom of taking stimulus money he usually relied on a few homely phrases: "You can't solve a problem caused by too much debt by piling on yet more debt"; "You're talking about a billion-dollar hole in the budget two years from now." The phrase "billion-dollar hole" always sounded weird to me (a hole worth a billion dollars?), and I doubt very many people understood what he meant by it. Anyhow he never had a cogent retort to the objection that the state had a right to its share of the cash and if we didn't take it somebody else would.

For a lot of people, though, that argument was beside the point. These people had become frightened by the prospect of wanton government spending and generational debt, and here was a man who, in apparent violation of his own political interests, was saying No. He already had the reputation of saying No to his state's legislature, to his own party, to federal bullying; now he was saying it again, only this time everybody seemed to be awake and listening.

The governor's enemies in the legislature thought they sensed weakness. The disputed $700 million, to be spent over two years, would mostly go to education, both K–12 and public colleges. About $37 million, if I remember, would go to law enforcement and prisons, and a few million to other, small-fry programs. But the bulk was meant for education, and education is, of course, the one thing nobody likes to oppose funding for. Over the previous few months, as the governor made clear his opposition to the stimulus, there had been talk about schools having to lay off teachers, of schools in poor rural areas becoming even more ramshackle than they already were, and of districts cutting science and arts programs. In an important sense, all this talk was purely irrational. For a variety of reasons, when people think about forgoing federal money—that is, of going without federal funding that might have been available under different circumstances—they think of it as a cut. The fact that it isn't a cut at all becomes immaterial; suddenly everyone is bemoaning budget reductions that haven't happened and won't happen. In any case, nobody really believed teachers would lose their jobs if the governor turned down the stimulus money. Members of the legislature would starve every agency in state government before they'd open themselves to the criticism that they had let teachers be laid off. Even so, it seemed almost everybody felt that the governor's intention to turn down stimulus money would somehow result in the widespread firing of teachers.

This time he had gone too far. The ones who supported the president's stimulus bill denounced him as an obstructionist, an ideologue, an out-of-touch millionaire; the ones who thought the stimulus bill was a terrible idea said that, although it was a terrible idea, the governor was foolish to turn away money when it would go to some other state if it didn't come to ours. I remember listening to one state senator, a member of the minority who wasn't known for speaking much on the floor, making a fervent plea to the governor to take the money. "We understand, Governor," he said. "We understand. The stimaluss is bad physical policy. Nobody disagrees with you. Least not the people I represent. But the stimaluss is the law o' the land. Can't nobody change that, and if we don't take that money, it's gon' go to Arkansas or Nebraska or Timbuktu."

On a long afternoon in late March we sat watching these and other speeches on the press office television. There'd already been a series of editorials and op-eds, some of them in the national papers, either ridiculing or reprobating the governor for heartlessness, foolishness, or insanity. The day before, the *New York Times* had editorialized against him. "It would be best, therefore," the *Times* concluded in its characteristic editorialese, for the governor "to find a face-saving way to reverse himself. If he does not, voters should remember that their governor placed politics ahead of schoolchildren and the schools that are struggling to save them." Somebody turned the television to cable news, and the condemnation was there too. There had been other governors who, back in February, had denounced the stimulus bill and said they didn't want the money, but most of them (maybe all of them by now) had gone silent. One of the news anchors was having a pleasant conversation with the station's news analyst, who was speaking of the governor as if his intention to turn down the stimulus money was evidence of a psychosis. "I mean," he was saying, "his state's got an unemployment rate of nine-point-five percent, the third highest in the nation. Whether he appreciates the gravity of his state's economic situation, or exactly what he's thinking—maybe he's not able to focus—anyway it's just a little unclear at this point." He said it with a smirk.

Stewart, who'd been leaning back in his chair, lunged forward and spouted a series of profanities at the television. A couple of the words I'd never even heard before.

Paul said, "I don't mean to state the obvious here, but we're arguing over seven hundred million dollars. Sorry, but the Department of Education could piss away seven hundred million in a week."

Gil had walked in and did a few high-fives. "This is all good, though, man. Did y'all see that the *New York Times* slammed the governor yesterday?"

"No, Gil," Nat said irritably, "we didn't see it. This is the governor's press office and no one here had any idea the *New York Times* ran an editorial about the governor yesterday."

"It's all good, though, man. It's all good. Our peeps love it. Do you realize," Gil said with an uncharacteristic air of gravity, "that in Chinese the word for 'crisis' and the word for 'opportunity' are the same word? I mean, this looks bad for us, for the governor. But we could use it."

Nat: "Hey, that's fascinating, Gil. And did you know, in English, your name and the word 'dumbass' are the same word?"

Stewart's laugh shook the room.

"Gil's got a point," someone said. "That's pretty much why

the Cultural Revolution was allowed to happen. Ten million dead, all because they were all saying 'opportunity' when they should have been saying 'crisis.'"

"Gil," Stewart said, still convulsing, "this is the press office. These guys live on bits of pseudo-wisdom like that one. They use them, they invent them."

"No, but let's be fair to Gil here," Nat said. "I was thinking about this yesterday. The Greeks had three words for 'love,' whereas we only have one. No, seriously. One of them means 'brotherly love'; one of them means the kind of love between a man and a woman. And then there's the word 'phileo.' It means 'love,' but it's a special kind of love. Like the love Gil has for stupid bullcrap he finds on the Internet."

This went on for five or ten minutes. Gil just giggled.

Suddenly I found myself saying, "Gil's right, though."

Everybody waited for the joke. But I didn't have a joke.

"No, I just mean—all this hostility isn't a bad thing. It's an honorable thing, actually. It just means our guy isn't acting out of base self-interest. He's doing this because he should." I wasn't intending to say any of this; it just came out. "I mean, take a look at Harrell's press guy, or Leatherman's staff, or Knotts's. Their guys were against the stimulus as long as it was the thing to be against. A month and a half ago it was great to bash the president and talk about how he was going to bankrupt the country, about how there was all this irrelevant junk in the bill, designed to do people favors, just expensive thank-you notes to people or companies or whatever who'd done favors for the administration or for some high-powered fraudster in Congress. A month and a half ago all these guys were denouncing central planning and top-down economics and Keynesianism even though they didn't know what any of those words meant. But now, oh, right, the bill's passed, it's the law of the land, and they can't wait to get their filthy little paws on it. And conveniently enough, that about-face just happens to accord with the conventional wisdom of editorial boards. And, I guess, of the electorate. So all aboard the stimulus train, right? Well, our guy said No. Other guys in other states said No, but then when they found out about giant mounds of federal cash just waiting to be spent, well, maybe all this top-down stuff isn't such a bad idea, just this once. Our guy said No, and when it was a done deal and there wasn't anything more he could do about it, he still said No. It doesn't matter how many editorialists call him crazy or a 'prisoner to his ideology.' It doesn't matter how many people moan into the TV cameras about all the teachers who'll supposedly be laid off if he doesn't take the money. It doesn't even matter if he's wrong. None of it matters. He said No for a reason, that reason still applies, and his answer is still No. And if the voters don't like it, they should be careful who they vote for next time."

Everybody stared.

"Actually I can't really believe I'm saying any of this because most days I want to call the governor terrible names, but my point was just to say—what was it you said, Gil?—that what feels like a crisis isn't necessarily a crisis. Okay, it might not be much of an opportunity, but it's not a crisis. The governor's saying No, and it doesn't matter how many people tell him to say Yes, he's not going to do it. So who would you rather work for: some soulless blob like Bobby Harrell, or for our boss? I'll take the boss, every time. Even if he's wrong."

I must have spoken for long enough to let all the irony seep out of the room. I felt my face turning red. Nat mumbled, "Well said. Go team," and got back to work. The others changed the topic or walked out.

———

It was two or three days later, April 2. There had been talk of a rally by educators. The plan was for a crowd to march three blocks from the Department of Education building to the State House, and there protest the governor's refusal to accept federal money for the education budget.

We liked protests. They were always happening at the State House for one thing or another. You would walk outside to get some lunch or fresh air, and a small crowd would be waving posters and shouting slogans; usually you couldn't make out what the slogans were. The more orderly groups would set up a podium and maybe a loudspeaker, and one member of the crowd, sometimes as few as ten or fifteen people, would address the rest. Occasionally you'd see a young black man dressed as a Klansman; he was always shouting about something, and he wore giant placards bearing the words "Judge James Simmons committed FRAUD $ PERJURY and Senator McConnell is trying 2 cover it up!" Once, I saw a single protester speaking at a podium; he was exercised about something, but there was no one within fifty yards of him.

Any time there was a large protest, "large" meaning more than forty people or so, we would walk outside and have a look. Sometimes we'd hear people denouncing the governor in strident terms. This had a way of lifting our spirits.

The protest on April 2 was supposed to be big; there had been an AP brief on it the day before. Stewart, Nat, and I stepped outside to watch. A podium and loudspeaker were set up, and various bystanders and security officers stood about. From high atop the State House steps, a few General Assembly members and their staff nonchalantly looked down, trying to figure out if the event merited their presence.

Ten or fifteen minutes went by, and we heard a drumbeat and whistles. Then, slowly, the crowd made its way through the manicured gardens of the east side of the State House and gathered in front of the podium. Over the course of twenty minutes the crowd grew to, I guessed, about a thousand people. Many of them were waving pink pieces of paper and shouting the words "Pink slip for the governor!"

As the crowd grew, the suit-wearing lawmakers and staffers gradually made their way down the steps, shyly at first, like coyotes approaching a carcass, but then more deliberately toward the podium. A variety of orators took turns at the microphone before the first of the politicians. Senator John Land, the man who'd been in the legislature longer than any other member, approached the lectern. The dislike between Land and the governor was not of the legendary kind, as it was between Knotts or Leatherman and the governor, but it was real; the governor had once removed Land's son, Cal, from the board of a state-owned electric utility, and Land the Elder had responded by slipping into a bill a provision divesting the governor of any power to remove board members. Slowly Land adjusted the microphone upward—he was a tall man—and scanned the multitude. The grin he always wore grew wider, and he said, "Well, glory!" The crowd cheered; Land beamed. Behind him his colleagues from the senate, Jakie Knotts and a few others, laughed uproariously at everything he said.

To one side of the crowd, though, was an antiprotest protest. There were no more than twenty-five of them. They were doing their best to mix their defiant chants in with the rest.

"Look at these two crowds," Nat said. "What would you say the difference is between them?"

I thought about the contrast.

"Pink slip for the governor! Pink slip for the governor!"

"Look at their people," Stewart said, pointing to the pink slip–waving educators. "There's a sameness about them. Middle-aged women, mostly. A few men, all with facial hair. They're all public school teachers and principals and district managers. Now look at our people."

There were a few hippies, a few Confederates; a woman with hair down to her backside holding up a sign—what did it say?—"Public education harms our children." There was a guy wearing a red, white, and blue satin jacket with a giant eagle head on the back; no satin jackets among the education crowd. There was a white man with an East Asian wife and three or four of their children skipping about. There was a black man with a chain wrapped around him.

"Yeah," Nat said, "what's the chain mean?"

"I don't know," Stewart replied, "something about en-slavement to debt, maybe? The point is, our people aren't some undifferentiated mass. They're crazy, but they're fun. They're human and they're alive. You can work with them. You can work with a guy who's willing to wrap a chain around his body to make some point understood only to himself. You can work with a Harley-riding redneck who probably wants us to secede from the Union. I mean, at least the guy isn't desperate to fit in. What I can't work with is a bunch of sanctimonious public employees who think the fate of Western civilization hinges on whether the education bureaucracy gets its hands on another seven hundred million dollars."

"Pink slip for the governor! Pink slip for the governor!"

"Completely agree with that, Stewart," Nat said. "The only problem is, we've got, what, twenty people? And there's about a thousand in the pink slip crowd."

Stewart: "Right about now would be a great time for the silent majority to get off its ass and make some noise."

11

~ TEA PARTY

I t was two weeks later, at around 10:30 A.M., and already you could hear the throb of a bass line coming from outside. A week before the governor had agreed to speak at a tax day rally on the State House grounds. When preparing remarks I usually tried to phone whoever was in charge of the event to figure out what sorts of things might be appropriate for the governor to say. For this event there was no such person, or rather the person supposedly in charge didn't know much about it. Who have you invited? I asked. "Everyone I could think of." Everyone? "Everyone." Is there a speaking order? "Not exactly." Anybody else organizing it? "Not that I know of." Are you advising media? "No, but they know about it. I reckon they'll be there." Any idea what people might like to hear from the governor? "Whatever he wants to say."

He called it a "tea party." People had been talking about tax day tea parties for a few weeks. Suddenly talk of debts and deficits was everywhere. You heard the word "trillion" more than you ever had before. The stimulus bill had passed, its final price tag coming to $830 billion. The banks and automakers had been bailed out; indeed one of the automakers had just been "reorganized" and partially taken over by the federal government. A bill that would give the federal government vast powers over the health insurance market was in the making. Many people felt the United States had in just one year become something like a European social democracy. That was fine if you thought social democracy a good and noble thing, but if you didn't, you were scared. It had happened so fast. Lehman Brothers went under, an election happened, and suddenly Congress wasn't just debating but was passing legislation you didn't think possible in America.

There was a feeling that the tea party rally might be a big deal, and in a rooting-for-the-underdog sort of way I hoped it would be, although it sounded gimmicky. At eleven o'clock I went outside to look around. On the north side of the State House there were already a couple thousand people milling about, which made me nervous. I'd written remarks for the governor a week before, but I was pretty sure he hadn't looked at them, since for all he knew he'd be talking to ten people.

I trotted back inside. The governor hadn't arrived from

the mansion yet. "Do you know if he's looked at the stuff I gave him for today?" I asked Shelby and Frances, the schedulers. They usually had a sense of whether he'd thought about what he wanted to say. They didn't think he had. "Can you call him and tell him there are at least three thousand people here?"

"Is that true?" Frances asked.

"Probably closer to a thousand. But just tell him three thousand to stress him out. He needs to start going over what he's going to say."

Shelby called him; she compromised and said "like two thousand."

He arrived about thirty minutes later. I was waiting at my desk. By this time I had learned to give him three or four options for any one event—not a single prepared text but a series of potential lines of thought. Usually I kept one of those narratives in reserve—in my head—so that if he stormed into the press office and announced his hatred of everything I'd written, which still happened occasionally, I could blurt out something as if it had just occurred to me. I learned that from Nat.

That is what happened around eleven-thirty on April 16, only in this instance he called me into his office.

"Wwwww," he said, looking at the material I'd put in his speech book.

He wanted me to say something so he could interrupt and tell me how nothing I'd written was any good, but today I thought I'd force him to initiate the conversation.

"Wwwww. Wwwhat is all this? This is nothing I can use."

"Do you have any thoughts about what—."

"How many people are out there?"

"I don't know, maybe five thousand."

"Okay, give me something I can use. Something about the founding fathers, or taxation without representation, or something. I mean, not that, but something like that."

Then, starting to walk out, I pretended to recall something important. "Okay, wait," I said. "That reminds me—something I saw."

"What?" he asked.

"Wait—where was it?—okay, I think I got it."

"What?"

It was definitely working.

"I don't know why I'm just thinking of this, but it's perfect."

"Come on, what?"

"Just a couple of blocks away, in the cemetery of the First Presbyterian Church, there's a gravestone. The name on it is John Calvert. It says, 'At the Liberty Tree, Charleston, 1766, he pledged to resist British taxation.'" Those are the precise words on the gravestone, but I said, "Or something like that."

He paused, which was a good sign. But then he asked, "I mean, so what?"

"So what? So here was a guy, an American patriot, a citizen of this state, whose whole life could be summed up by the stand he took in Seventeen-sixty-six, by the stand he took against unjust taxation and unjust governmental power. And his gravestone's three blocks from here. It's perfect."

"Wwwwwhat's the liberty tree?"

"I don't know. They planted liberty trees back then. It just signified liberty taking root or something. They did it in the French Revolution too. I guess it was at some meeting place for patriots in Charleston."

"I can't go out there talking about the liberty tree in Charleston if I don't know what it was," he said.

"Yes you can. Nobody's gonna care. It was a tree where people met and talked about liberty. It symbolized the growth of liberty. Whatever, it doesn't matter. What matters—."

"Find me something on the liberty tree."

"The tree isn't the point."

"Find me—something—on—the liberty tree. Hurry. I've got to be out there in ten minutes."

Defeat. I enlisted a couple of my colleagues to get some information about liberty trees. Chris, who'd joined the press office a few months before, found something about a judge in Charleston digging up the roots of the liberty tree, which the British had burned, and fashioning the handle of a cane out of one of the pieces and sending it to Thomas Jefferson.

When we walked outside, we weren't prepared for what we saw. The whole northern half of the State House grounds teemed with dissenters, not just in the public area in front of the steps but among the trees and shrubs all the way to Gervais Street. It was as if that little band of jolly malcontents protesting the pink-slippers had mated and multiplied. The governor walked slowly through the crowd, his coatless white shirt gleaming in the sun. Leather-bedecked motorcyclists shook his hand and smiled, huddles of flip-flop–wearing students shouted his name, and white-headed men in ties spoke into his ear, then slapped him gently on the back as he made his way toward the microphone. There were men wearing colonial wigs and women with bonnets and giant hoop petticoats. A band of youth (homeschoolers, I assumed) played patriotic songs on flutes and drums. One man had the words of the Preamble printed in black letters on his white shirt and trousers; another played "The Star Spangled Banner" on a saxophone. Families stopped the governor for a picture; one of them had three little girls, the littlest of whom wore a T-shirt bearing the phrase "Mommy's little tax exemption."

When he stepped onto the dais, twenty minutes after the scheduled time, the crowd erupted.

He began nervously. "Aaahh. Ah I won't take much of y'all's time, but I did want to talk for just a minute on this larger notion of why it's important that we water the tree of liberty."

The masses erupted again. He went on to talk about how the present moment is a "gut check moment in American history," which was his own weird variation on the typical politician's "crossroads" metaphor ("We're at a crossroads in American history"). It was hard to hear what he was saying; the sound quality was bad, and he seemed unsure of what he meant. He talked about the "all-seeing eye" on the one-dollar bill (he'd borrowed the dollar from a staffer) to make some point he'd heard or read before but that no one understood. Aaron shot a questioning look at me and I shot one back.

But the cheers got louder. Verbal inelegance didn't matter. Incoherence didn't matter. The crowd was applauding the man and his reputation.

After the governor and a few others had spoken, a young man approached me. By appearance he was East Asian, but he spoke with a midwestern American accent. "You work for the governor?" he asked. He handed me a large envelope. Inside, he said, was a picture of the governor with him and his dad. They had met at some occasion in Chicago. There was a stamped envelope inside. Would I get the governor to sign it and just drop it in the mail? "My dad will flip out when he sees this," he said.

I asked him why somebody from up north cared about the governor of a little southern state. "Oh, you know why," he said, as if I were teasing him.

"No, I don't."

"When he spoke to our group—or my father's group, really—I'd never heard anything like it. I mean, it wasn't delivery or anything. I'm a student at Penn, okay, and we get great speakers all the time. But I grew up in Chicago, and my dad's really active in the party there. He came and spoke to my dad's group, okay. It's just that I'd never heard a politician talk that honestly, without any of the polish or the b.s. Usually politicians talk about how great things will be once they get their hands on the power. You know, they're gonna turn everything around. He just like talked about how spending as a proportion of GDP has risen too high too fast, and it isn't sustainable anymore, and how spending borrowed money is devaluing the currency, you know, and how basically even under the best of circumstances, we're all in trouble—liberals, conservatives, all of us. Just totally realistic, that guy. And now he's the only guy who's willing to actually turn down the stimulus money.

Not to like just talk about how bad it is, but to actually turn it down. I mean—you know all this."

"Yeah. So you drove all the way from Pennsylvania to see him?"

"Well, my brother works in Raleigh. But yeah, when I heard about this, I drove down."

Later it occurred to me that this young man had hit on something important. The governor's heroism, or people's perception of it, which comes to the same thing, consisted in his brutal honesty about the limits of what could be done. It was a kind of antiheroism, but it was heroism all the same, because telling people what they cannot do takes greater mettle than telling them what they can do.

———

Session ended that year with the customary barrage of budget vetoes, and as usual the legislature overrode most of them. This time, though, one of the vetoes included $350 million in federal stimulus money, the first half of the $700 million. The fight over stimulus money finally ended in early June, when the state supreme court forced the governor to apply for the funds on the grounds that the General Assembly had appropriated them. We were all sick of the word "stimulus."

At the end-of-session party at the mansion, the governor gathered everyone around and gave a characteristically awkward talk about how we were all making a difference for the sake of our children and grandchildren. He said more or less the same thing he'd said the two or three years before (and wore the same blue gingham shirt and blue jeans he'd worn the two or three years before). "It only takes one person to shatter a whole system. Just one person refusing to go along to get along. Think about Rosa Parks. This group is that one person. It's not about me. It's about this administration saying, 'Hold on, let's think about this before we keep going.'" This year, though, he added a line at the end: "This is about more than this state. This is about the direction we're headed in as a country."

12

I t was a Thursday. The governor was leaving town and wanted to see me and Chris about something before he left. We sat silently outside his office, where the schedulers' desks were, and June's. We often sat there looking like a pair of schoolboys waiting outside the headmaster's office for corporal punishment. Chris looked unhappy; he once compared one of the governor's fiercer tirades with being "shot in the face." He would go on to be a highly successful television news producer, but he didn't flourish in this job; he liked to edit copy, not produce it.

"It's your birthday?" I asked June. There was a cake on Frances's desk that said "Happy Birthday June." It hadn't been cut, and the candles hadn't been lit.

"Sure is," June said. "On Saturday. These young things thought it would be nice to remind me of it."

Just then the governor's meeting ended and a few people filed out.

I put my head through the door. "You wanted to see me and Chris, sir?"

He motioned for us to come in.

"Wwwwait a minute," he said, fiddling through papers. "Okay, I'm going out of town for a few days, and I want you guys to work on some arguments. Big picture arguments." Now he looked at the ceiling, as if he could see these arguments. "The federal government's essentially devaluing the currency, going further into debt by printing money and trying to manage the national economy. I know other economies have tried to do that. Disasters. Think of Weimar Germany. I don't know. Argentina in the nineteen-eighties. Find some historical instances where government spending took above a certain percentage of GDP—I don't know what the percentage is, maybe forty, fifty percent. Britain in the seventies. Japan now. I don't know. Whatever you can find. Books. Magazine articles. Nothing too technical. But I want it boiled down. Don't just give me a book and say 'Here, read it.' I'm reading a stack of books as it is. I need to have a deeper understanding of this stuff if I'm going to try and pitch it to a bigger audience, and I need to be able to put it in terms that everybody can understand."

Chris glanced at me when he said "bigger audience."

We scribbled everything down as he spoke, and after another four or five minutes we were done. Chris and I walked out. I stopped at Frances's desk to ask about something or other.

The governor walked out of his office a few seconds later. He was about to say something to Lewis, his personal assistant, when he caught sight of the cake. "Oh," he said, almost inaudibly.

Then, with four or five of us watching in silence, he walked over to the cake, mumbled the words, "Eat this tonight," picked up a knife, then cut a corner out of the cake and put it on one of the paper plates. He took the cake into his office and shut the door.

Frances sat with her eyes wide, her mouth gaping. "Did he just do that?"

"I'm sorry," June said with a disbelieving smile, "did he just cut my cake and not even wish me Happy Birthday?"

Later the staff gathered and sang "Happy Birthday" to June, presenting her with a cake with a corner missing.

———

The governor wasn't yet leading the national opposition to the president, but he was elbowing his way to the front. Invitations to more and better speaking events were coming in all the time, and more and more well-known television journalists wanted to talk to him or have him on their show.

One Saturday afternoon I was talking to a neighbor as our children played together. He asked me what it was like to work for the governor. I stammered for a moment and came out with something that didn't make much sense. My neighbor said, "He just seems like—I don't know—like he doesn't enjoy being governor very much."

———

When I think back to that summer, I can't remember any sunlight. In fact there was plenty of it; I mean actual, literal sunlight. I just don't remember any. I feel now as if I spent the entire three months in that tiny press office, with great stacks of newspapers all around and sterile fluorescent light shining from above. The days were long, but they were spent entirely (it now seems) indoors, tapping out press statements and fielding calls from famous journalists and angry constituents and poring over photocopies of flight manifests. Not writing speeches. That summer I wrote no speeches, no talking points.

In the afternoons I often had coffee with Stella. She'd been hired as some kind of computer guru on the strength of having come from San Diego. Stella rode her bike to work, wore flip-flops and brown and black clothes, and refused to take orders. She probably should have been fired on many occasions. The governor would tell her to do something slightly improper and she would tell him, directly, as if she were a defiant daughter talking to a timorous father, "No." (All politicians from time to time direct their staff to do things that, technically, as public employees, they shouldn't do. Nothing terrible or even scandalous, just improper: make a photo album for the politician's daughter, deliver a bowl of chicken salad to a party hosted by the first lady.) The governor would call Stella, and she would ignore the call—it was wonderful. Somehow, though, she couldn't be fired. This wasn't because she was young and chirpy and beautiful, as the schedulers were; Stella was sufficiently attractive but not eye candy like them. Yet there was something about her that made the thought of treating her roughly, even when she deserved it, unthinkable.

One afternoon in June she asked if I had heard anything. I hadn't. Stella's desk was near Stewart's and she often overheard things.

"SLED put an APB out on the governor." SLED was the State Law Enforcement Division.

"They lost him?"

"I guess so. That's why you put out APBs."

The governor was always slipping away from his protection detail. Some high-level politicians cultivate the "entourage look," as Lewis called it. They like to be surrounded by men in dark suits and wearing earpieces; they must feel it makes them look presidential. The governor of Texas was notorious for his entourage at National Governors Association meetings. A ring of Rangers surrounded him wherever he went. I was told by a colleague who'd just come back from an NGA meeting that a reporter had tried to get past the Rangers to ask him a question and they knocked her down.

Our governor, by contrast, was always telling his security detail to stand some distance away, which in some settings made their job extremely difficult; sometimes, without telling anybody on the detail, he went out to a hardware store or on a bike ride by himself.

"That's fantastic," I said. "He's always giving them the slip."

"No," Stella said, "I don't think it's fantastic. Not this time. SLED wouldn't put out an APB unless he was really gone. Like gone gone. Lost, nowhere to be found."

"Maybe he's dead," I said, laughing. "Sorry. I didn't mean that."

"He could be. But I think he might have gone crazy."

I still wanted to laugh, but I could see she was serious, which was unusual. And I knew she had a point. He had been acting oddly even by his own standards. A week before he had scheduled a trip to Washington to attend what anybody would regard as a highly important event to which he'd been invited to speak; he had put long hours into the talk he'd planned to give, but then at the last minute he decided not to go because he was "sick," which he manifestly was not. Just a few days before that, he'd come into the press office and given me a sheet of paper. He wanted me to file it. We often filed material he thought might be useful for speeches, and sometimes this included notes he'd jotted down. "It's important," he said. "Don't lose it." After he walked out, I read it. On a plain piece of notebook paper he had written, "Once upon a time there were 3 little pigs & the time came for them to leave home and seek their fortunes. Before they left—their mother told them—whatever you do, do it the best you can because that's the way to get along in the world."

"What if he's gone off somewhere, and just lost it?" Stella asked.

"He's a bit too calculating, don't you think, to lose sanity altogether?"

———

Later that day reporters started calling, asking where the governor was. Aaron asked why they wanted to know. Because, they said, Jakie Knotts called them and told them to call and ask.

Apart from what I'd heard from Stella, I hadn't heard anything spoken openly about the governor's whereabouts, so I asked Aaron how Knotts knew to ask.

"Because someone at SLED leaked it to him. He's got friends there."

I waited for more, but Aaron said nothing. So I said, "I don't mean to be a pest, but—um—."

"But do we know where he is?"

"Yeah," I said. "Do we?"

"No," he answered. "He's supposed to be on some kind of hiking trip. But we haven't been able to get in touch with him. To be honest, I don't care where he is. I get a lot more done when he's gone. And it's a lot pleasanter when he's gone. Do you care where he is?"

"No, I like it much better. I think he should stay gone all the time."

On Wednesday morning his absence was above-the-fold headline material: "Where's the Governor?" "Governor Goes Missing." "Governor AWOL." Someone from *The State* had contacted the first lady, who said matter-of-factly that she didn't know where he was. No one in the office took her comment that seriously; we all knew he liked to go off by himself. I remember hearing someone say that the governor liked to be in front of the crowd or not in the crowd at all, at the center of attention or totally absent from it.

The night before, a little after ten o'clock, Aaron had sent out a press statement—not a release, just a four-sentence statement—about where the governor was. He'd been "hiking on the Appalachian Trail," the statement said. "The governor called to check in with his chief of staff this morning. It would be fair to say the governor was somewhat taken aback by all of the interest this trip has gotten. Given the circumstances and the attention this has garnered, he communicated to us that he plans on returning to the office tomorrow."

Early that morning Aaron, Stewart, Nat, and a few others were in the press office. By the time I got there, around eight-thirty, they were debating whether the boss was a bastard for leaving without making it clear where he was going or was entitled to go wherever he wanted without telling anybody because it didn't matter if the governor of an insignificant state couldn't be reached instantly by phone.

After about ten o'clock I didn't see Stewart or Aaron any more. Reporters were everywhere. Most of them I'd never seen. Some of them I'd seen on the national networks and cable news channels. Cameramen lugged their equipment around the State House rotunda. It was all pretty amusing; they'd come all the way down here from Washington and New York because they thought they'd see some sordid southern tale, but all they'd see is a governor who, in addition to the typical politician's need to soak up attention from everyone, also liked to be alone and unreachable.

I saw Nat in the hall. "Do you know what's going on?" he asked me.

"I never know what's going on."

"The place is crawling with reporters, and Aaron's no-where. Stewart's nowhere. Something's definitely not right."

"What's not right," I said in an attempt to be reassuring, "is that the governor is a self-absorbed jackass who doesn't have the decency to tell his chief of staff where he is even though half the world is asking."

"Yeah, I heard the London *Telegraph* called."

"They did."

"Great. I'm telling you, something's going very wrong."

"You've said that many times before," I said.

"Which means I'm bound to be right this time."

———

Aaron called around noon. "Lots of people calling?"

"Yeah," I said. "What's going on?"

"We're doing a press conference in the rotunda at one o'clock."

"What's he going to say?"

"That's all I can tell you. Just tell media it's at one."

"This is bad, isn't it?"

"Yeah."

I hung up and told Chris about the press conference.

He responded, in a singsong falsetto voice, "Awesome."

For forty-five minutes we answered phone calls from journalists and told them there was a press conference at one o'clock but that we couldn't say what it was about for the excellent reason that we didn't know what it was about. Around fifteen minutes before one, June walked in. Her eyes were red and glistened with tears. She was about to speak, but paused. We waited. Then she said, "The governor is about to say something that's"—again she paused—"going to be disappointing." And she walked quickly out.

———

When the governor had a press conference in the rotunda of the State House, we usually prepared for it pretty thoroughly. We'd coordinate with the reporters and camera crews, ensure the podium was in the right place, have releases ready to hand out, and so on. This time it all happened on its own. I just stood in the crowd and tried to look grave and well-informed, but I also tried to eavesdrop on the reporters' conversations in an attempt to figure out what was going on. But they were as clueless as I was. The man in the Mets cap was there, gazing up at the lightbulbs; he knew as much as I did.

At last the governor came through the entrance of the west wing of the State House. All the talking and bustle quieted down. We all stared at him as he walked slowly forward. He walked gracefully as always, but as he passed me I saw in his face an expression of fear that I'd never seen there before. He tried to mumble "Hello" and "How are you?" to people he recognized, but his eyes were large, maybe swollen, and they'd lost that appearance of cool omniscience I'd seen so often before. He looked like a man about to ask for mercy from a stern judge.

He began by saying he'd be brief and to the point but then started talking about "adventure trips" he'd taken as a teenager. He stammered and talked almost inaudibly; I could hardly follow him. I thought for a moment that he'd been caught in some act of corruption. Then I heard him say, "I've been unfaithful to my wife."

I've never been able to bear too much truth at one time, and from this point I didn't register much. "It started out as these things often do, as a dear friendship," he was saying, and I felt an overwhelming desire to lie down, alone, and think about nothing. I walked back to my desk and put my head down. I could still hear everything he was saying because we'd left Fox News on—"I hurt her, I hurt my wife," click-click-click went the cameras—but I didn't comprehend.

Bridget put her hand on my shoulder and said, "It's gon' be all right, baby. I know it hurts. He's a piece o' work as it is, and now this. Lord. But it's gon' be all right. Remember, the Lord knows."

Over the next few hours, as colleagues gathered in the press office to express a variety of opinions about what had happened, I kept quiet and gathered the essential facts. He had been in Buenos Aires, not on the Appalachian Trail. His mistress was named Maria. A reporter with *The State* had gotten a tip that he was on a flight from Buenos Aires to Atlanta, and she'd confronted him as he stepped into the terminal. The first lady had known about it for some time and fiercely disapproved. He'd said in the press conference that he'd spent the "last five days crying in Argentina," which we all agreed was an unfortunate way of putting it.

He was not resigning, not immediately anyhow.

"Still," Aaron said, "it won't hurt to start looking around, boys."

"You think they'll impeach him?" Nat asked.

Someone said they'd been looking for an excuse to bury him for seven years and that this would give them their chance.

Paul, now the head of policy, sat on the edge of a desk looking cross and silently throwing a rubber ball against the wall. It was odd to see him silent. Paul was one of the world's great interrupters; when he wanted to tell you something, he didn't care what you were doing or who you were talking to at the time. It was an odd trait in a southerner. Later I learned his father was from Cincinnati.

At last someone asked Paul what he was thinking. He stopped throwing the ball against the wall. Then he threw it one more time and said, "Could somebody explain to me why he couldn't just admit what he'd done and shut up? Why couldn't he just say, 'Okay, so I was down in South America with this girl. Woman, whatever. I'm sorry. I lied. I said I was going hiking, but I went to see her.' Done. Why couldn't he just say that? Why couldn't he just shut his hole?"

Nat: "Because he—. You can't just—. We should have—."

Someone asked if anybody had seen Stewart.

"He's in his office," Aaron said. "He's a little upset."

The thought of Stewart being upset put a stop to the chatter. It didn't seem possible that Stewart could be shaken by anything, not by anything the boss did. During the press conference the governor had evidently made it insufficiently clear that his staff, namely Stewart and Aaron, had not intentionally misled journalists but had simply relayed what he had told them about his whereabouts. When the press conference was over, Stewart, Aaron, and Rick Wilken (the previous chief of staff and a longtime friend of the governor) had followed the boss into his office. The result of this conference was a press statement making it clear that no one had deliberately lied for the governor. What happened in that meeting became the subject of rumor and legend; one version had Stewart—or perhaps it was Aaron—picking up a manila folder full of papers and throwing it hard, straight at the governor. Supposedly the folder curved upward into the air and came down in a shower of paper all around the governor as he sat looking angry and helpless at his desk.

That story is almost certainly untrue, but in the days that followed, when I'd sense keenly the pointlessness of everything I was doing, I'd think of that paper cascade falling around the governor, and it would make me smile. For years some of us had secretly imagined—we all knew how improbable it was, but it wasn't impossible—the governor accepting his party's nomination for the presidency. I had imagined him waving to great throbbing crowds in some vast arena, confetti falling all around. Now he was just a brooding sad-eyed failure of a politician with a few sheets of paper falling haphazardly over his head.

13

IMPEACHMENT

The next morning I woke up and thought I'd had a terrible dream. I know that's a predictable thing to say, but it's true. As slowly I realized what had happened, I got up and went to get the paper. I happened to notice on my desk Douglas Brinkley's biography of Rosa Parks. I'd just started reading it with the intention of finding good speech material—one of a great many efforts that now seemed pointless.

Everything we'd worked for was discredited; everything the administration aimed to achieve in its second term was at an end. Now we were either out of a job or bound to spend the next year cleaning up the dirty mess of an irrelevant politician. And yet I felt somehow liberated. I walked into the office that morning without wanting to vomit or turn around and go home. Everything was pointless now, so why care about it? Now it was at least funny.

That day's *State* newspaper had reprinted several emails between the governor and his mistress. Evidently the paper's editors had had these emails for some time but didn't publish them for lack of corroborating evidence, evidence he had given them when one of the newspaper's reporters caught him coming back into the country from Buenos Aires. The emails themselves were all the things one would expect of correspondence between two middle-aged lovers in a secret affair—shallow, pretentiously worldly wise, cloying—but apart from one or two references to body parts, they weren't dirty. The worst thing about them, for me, was that I couldn't help feeling I'd written them myself. They were laden with words and phrases from my list, which I hardly bothered to consult anymore, so thoroughly had I internalized it. "You are special and unique and fabulous in a whole host of ways that are worth a much longer conversation." "You have a level of sophistication that is so fitting with your beauty." "In this regard it is action that goes well beyond the emotion of today." "If you have pearls of wisdom on how we figure all this out please let me know."

There was to be a cabinet meeting the following morning; whether it had been scheduled beforehand or called for the purpose I don't remember. Reporters and cameramen were everywhere. I'd made my way through them on the way in, and several had asked where the meeting would be. It was to be in a building adjacent to the State House, which meant the governor would have to walk through one of two public areas: either through the rotunda, where the press conference had been the day before, or outdoors across the grounds. Somehow the governor had already gotten into the office that morning, and now hundreds of these hounds waited at both exit points.

At last he left, choosing the outdoor route. I followed at a distance. This great mob, with boom poles protruding from it, camera lights glaring, moved slowly across the grounds, with the governor at its center. He looked tired and exasperated, as if he'd been kept awake all night by people laughing at him. His eyes were red, his hair ungroomed and in need of a trim. Now and again he appeared to mumble something in response to a question.

I watched the meeting on television; all the cable channels ran it live. Gil and a few others came in to watch. He began with the second of hundreds of apologies. "I let each of you down," he said to the agency heads present. "And for that I again apologize. But I've been doing a lot of soul searching on that front, and what I find interesting is the story of David. And the way in which, aahh, he fell mightily; fell in very, very significant ways, but then picked up the pieces and went from there. And it really began with, first of all, a larger quest that I think is well-expressed in the Book of Psalms, on the notion of humility—humility toward others, humility in one's own spirit."

"Did he just compare himself to David?" someone asked.

"Dude," Gil said, stretching, "that's a bad analogy. David was killed by his son."

"No he wasn't, you idiot."

"Uh-hut!"

An hour or so later we were all still there, wondering if we should do any work. Even basic duties seemed pointless. On the news channels talking heads were ridiculing the boss every half hour or so. The papers were full of columns comparing him to other fallen politicians. Suddenly the governor, Nat, and Stewart walked in. "Would y'all excuse us please? Except for you," he said pointing to me.

When the door was closed, the governor said to Nat and Stewart, "Go ahead."

"Okay, you can't compare yourself to David," Nat said.

"I wasn't comparing myself to David. I was just saying, wwwww, 'Here's a guy in the Bible, he did some bad stuff, there were some dire consequences, but he picked up the pieces and went forward.'"

I thought: He can't describe what he's done.

"Governor," Stewart said, in a slightly more deferential tone, "I admit, I don't know that much about the Bible, and neither do most people out there, but most people have a vague recollection from Sunday school that David killed a giant when he was like ten, wiped out the Philistines, and did a lot of other bad-ass stuff. And I'm pretty sure he's considered one of the greatest kings in the Old Testament, am I right? Anyhow, definitely one of history's great men."

"And he didn't just commit adultery," Nat said. "He had the woman's husband murdered."

I thought: He also repented.

"Wwwww."

"Governor," Nat said, "I get what you're trying to say, but

now's not the time to draw comparisons between yourself and the heroes of history."

"Wwwww."

"Look, if you—."

"Okay I get it, I get it," the governor said. "Bad analogy. So what I need you to do," he said to me, "is come up with a few examples from the Bible—or from history, or from whatever—that kind of show, you know, how when you've made a mess, you do the best you can to clean it up, you make it right the best you can, and you keep going. You don't just give up."

"What about Samson?" I suggested, remembering just as I said it that Samson killed himself and a lot of other people to "make it right."

"Wwwwhatever. Give me five to ten of them. Some stuff to react to."

———

Almost every working day for the next two months, something bad happened. One day the house caucus published a letter, signed by all but two or three of its members, urging the governor to resign. The next day the governor told the Associated Press that Maria had been his "soul mate" and that their relationship had been "tragic" and "forbidden" but a "love story" all the same. The next day we heard from the press that he had seen Maria during a state economic development trip to a variety of South American countries, thus "using taxpayer dollars to see his mistress." The next day a sometime ally in the legislature told the press he was preparing to introduce a bill of impeachment. The day after that the governor's wife announced she was moving out of the mansion and taking their sons. A day or two went by with no bad news, but then the AP ran a story about an email leaked to one of its reporters showing the governor pleading with some kind of "spiritual mentor," "I am committed to her [his wife] in a commitment sense, but my heart is just not alive here as it ought to be." Then *The State*, whose reporters had now scoured documents relating to the governor's travels, reported that he had once reimbursed himself for a flight he'd won at a charity auction. A couple of days later the first lady told Oprah Winfrey that her husband had asked permission to see his mistress one last time—releasing another round of commentary about the governor's cruelty and self-absorption—and the day after that *The State* ran a story about how he had flown business class while insisting that all other state employees fly coach. The day that last story ran you could hear Stewart walking around the office singing,

Put me in, coach!
I'm ready to play, today!

The governor had two things in his favor. The first was that the legislature wasn't in session. If it had been, impeachment would have come up quickly, and his enemies would have finished him off. The second was that the lieutenant governor was André Bauer. Bauer was the youngest lieutenant governor in state history, and he acted the part. He was known for showing up at bars and parties with a different twenty-year-old woman on his arm each time. He was young, midthirties, but he was one of those old-school politicians whose campaigns consist of a few badly made television ads and a million handshakes. He'd walk around, locking eyes with anyone within a ten-foot radius, saying, "How are you? Good to see you!" You had to admire his discipline. Like a lot of young up-and-coming politicians, though, he had lost the ability to seem authentic. He had vast energy but no sagacity. Once, he showed up at a homeless shelter to hand out blankets, only it was April and 70 degrees outside. Another time he showed up at a home for the elderly to hand out electric fans; it was late August.

More widely known were Bauer's misadventures behind the wheel—one resulting in a reckless driving charge, the next in a warning for speeding, and still another resulting in no charge at all for exceeding a hundred in a seventy-mile-per-hour zone. And during his reelection campaign he had crashed a plane apparently by the simple expedient of not knowing how to fly it. Neither instance suggested Bauer to be the possessor of wisdom. At the time of the governor's fall, I heard a great many people say they didn't favor resignation for the sole reason that André Bauer would become governor.

He wanted badly to be governor, though. On the morning of August 26 he announced a press conference at which he would "issue a major public statement concerning the ongoing investigation" of the governor at noon. Bauer had a marvelous talent for bad timing; Senator Ted Kennedy had died the day before. (Even when Bauer's timing wasn't bad, Aaron would make it bad. If the lieutenant governor scheduled a press conference for two o'clock, Aaron would intentionally send out a substantive release—say, the findings of some study committee—at eleven. Aaron did this, to his great credit, "just 'cause I hate him.")

At the press conference Bauer made an offer to the governor: If he would resign, Bauer would promise not to run for governor. "I lie awake at night thinking and worrying about the people of this state," he said with an expression of deep concern.

We scheduled our own press conference for a few hours later. The entire press corps trekked to the State House again just to hear the governor say he'd decided not to take Bauer's offer.

The verbiage became so thick that summer you could almost feel it. There were hundreds of letters to the editor about him, and they were in every paper: local papers, weekly papers, even community newsletters that ordinarily didn't deal with government and politics at all. A few of the letter writers took a measured tone, but most were outraged. The governor's behavior seemed to inject harebrained metaphors and crazy images into the air; people could hardly express themselves without choking on them. "This is a transparent smokescreen!" "The meat and potatoes of it, in a nutshell, is that our state is once again a laughingstock!" One letter I thought a memorable specimen. I have it before me now. "Governor, your time line is at hand," it says. "You have committed the ultimate sin. . . . 'Lust' was your driving force. So since you have been shown to be a 'dog,' wag your tail and keep on stepping . . . down, that is. . . . Take a good look in the mirror. The shoe hurts when it's on the other foot."

A week or so after the governor's "tearful confession," as reporters referred to it again and again, the letters had begun pouring into the Correspondence Office. There were far too many to respond to, as in normal circumstances we tried to do, but I responded to as many as I could. Some of them were nonsensical; most were kindly meant, with odd impractical exhortations; some were touching. One little girl wrote, "I have heard you in the news a lot. I am not sure why, but I heard some people do not want you to be the governor any more. I like you to stay as governor. My mom said you said you were sorry for what you did wrong. Did you told Jesus you were sorry? If Jesus can forgive you, then everyone else should also. You are a very good governor and I hope you stay."

In early August the legislature scheduled a special session on extending unemployment benefits, but the rumor was that Representative Greg Delleney intended to introduce articles of impeachment. Delleney, ordinarily an inconspicuous member from the northern part of the state, was a man not to be trifled with on the subject of moral behavior. I remember hearing Jeane say that he was one of the few members who didn't "fool around" when he came to the capital.

For several days Nat had been saying this would be the end. "There's no stopping it. For seven years the guys upstairs have hated him. He's insulted them, he's ignored them, he hasn't taken their calls, and he's exposed them. This is their chance to put him away, and I tell you they're gonna do it. And to tell you the truth I don't blame them."

"On what charge?"

"Dereliction of duty. He left the state without telling anyone where he was going. Not even Stewart knew."

"You're wrong," I said. "It doesn't matter if this little state doesn't have anybody in charge for a few days. Before cell phones—before phones—if the governor went up to Washington or some place, he'd be totally out of reach for two weeks."

"And he would have told everybody where he was going."

"What if he had a change of plans? He'd have to send letters telling everybody where he was off to, and that would take days."

I honestly didn't think they would impeach him for the simple reason that to impeach a governor is to take a political risk, and the vast majority of them wouldn't take serious risks. They would find a way to tut-tut and tell the world how inexcusable and reprehensible the governor's behavior had been, but they wouldn't actually put him out. They'd call it unacceptable and then accept it.

The governor had become obsessed with lists. He wanted a list of opinion writers who had defended him and a list of those who had ridiculed him, another of donors he needed to call to apologize for "letting them down," still another of Rotary Clubs he hadn't addressed in more than a year.

"Courson!" he might shout. He meant Senator John Courson. "What's Courson said about resignation?"

"Uh," one of us would say.

"Come on! We've got to know this. We need a list. Put together a list of every guy upstairs who's said something publicly about stepping down."

And off one of us would go—usually it was me—to compile another list. Nat wagered it wouldn't be long until he demanded a list of all our lists.

I'd compiled that list of house and senate members who supported resignation, and it was almost identical to the list of members of the legislature. Only two or three members of the caucus didn't put their name on a letter calling on the governor, for the good of the state, to step down.

That afternoon I walked up to the house gallery and waited for the session to start. The floor was packed, which was extremely unusual for a special session in the middle of summer called for the purpose of changing one law that virtually every member agreed needed to change. They were there for Delleney's motion, I thought.

Speaker Harrell oversaw the proceedings efficiently. It took no more than thirty minutes to get the final vote on the unemployment law.

"Is there any other business?" he asked.

Delleney rose. He had a thin, pronounced nose and neatly brushed brown hair, and with his determined expression I thought he looked like a bird of prey.

"Mr. Speaker," he said, "I've introduced articles relating to the governor's recent absence from the state. Rather than wait until January to address the matter, I would submit to my colleagues on both sides of the aisle that this is too important to be left for another six months. Mr. Speaker, I move we take it up now."

"Mr. Delleney," Harrell said, "this session has been called for one purpose only, and I'm finding it hard to see how your motion relates."

"Mr. Speaker, impeachment is something only the house can do," Delleney contended. "We act separately and independently from the senate in this process. We are the only ones that can impeach. I would submit that, in order to move forward on a subject as important as this one, the house should take it up now."

Harrell paused. "Mr. Delleney, your argument strikes me as tenuous, but I'm willing to entertain debate on the question. Is there debate on the question? Mr. McLeod."

Representative Walt McLeod, a tiny and ancient member, rose to his feet. As a member of the minority, McLeod had never been a "friendly," as Jeane called potential allies. I knew little about him other than that he liked occasionally to rant from the podium, always in a voice far louder than his tiny stature would signify and always concluding with the words "I thank the members for listening to this little tirade" or some similar charming apology.

"Mr. Speaker," McLeod said, "I just want to be clear. We came to the capital today to make a minor change to the law and extend unemployment benefits, and now we're being asked to take up the impeachment of a governor? Well, Mr. Speaker, as many of y'all know, I am no fan of the governor's policies. I bear him no ill will and once in a while I agree with what he says, but we don't see eye to eye on most things.

But I recognize that sometimes a man falls into folly, and it would do us all good to remember that we too have fallen, we too have been guilty of some mighty stupid things, and we don't necessarily want it brought before the world in this way. That's just my opinion. I know some differ. And anyway, I think bringing this up now, rather than waiting till the house has a better feel for what laws might or might not have been broken, if any, I don't know—Mr. Delleney may have some strong arguments later on, but at this point, his proposal is absolutely immatu—I mean, *pre*mature." McLeod paused, then looked around at Delleney. "Might even be *im*mature."

The house exploded in laughter.

Harrell, chuckling, asked if anyone else wished to debate the question.

There were two or three more questions, but by their tone it was pretty clear that the feeling of the house was against Delleney. I suppose members didn't want to take up impeachment because they didn't want to spend another two weeks or a month in town, though many of them bore such hatred for the governor that they would have made that sacrifice. I've always felt that Representative McLeod's slip of the tongue saved the governor's job, and mine.

14

⸙ A LARGER NOTION

Two or three months passed, and slowly I began writing again. Not op-eds or talking points, mainly just letters. There were lots of thank-you letters to write; far more, in fact, than before the scandal. Ordinarily people sent gifts—a map of Italy from the Italian consul in Atlanta, say, or a hand-crafted pen from prisoners at one of the state prisons—and these were all to get personal notes in response. Now there were more gifts, but they were mostly of a particular kind: the mail bin was full of books with titles like *The Key to Companionship* and *Your Life, Your Marriage.* One was called, improbably, *The History and Philosophy of Marriage.* Another—this one self-published, it appeared—bore the imposing title *Understanding the Devastating Effects of*

Sex Outside of Marriage. Initially I thought these had been sent by pranksters, and maybe some of them had been, but I read the notes accompanying them and the senders seemed to be genuinely, if a little unctuously, concerned. One of the notes began, "I foolishly destroyed my marriage many years ago. If I had read this book, I might have done things differently." A great many well-meaning supporters thought the governor would benefit from watching a movie called *Fireproof*. ("Lt. Caleb Holt lives by the old firefighter's adage: Never leave your partner behind. Inside burning buildings, it's his natural instinct. In the cooling embers of his marriage, it's another story.") At one point there were at least fifty copies of the movie lying in a pile; staffers were told to take as many as they pleased.

The governor himself dictated a few responses to these well-wishers, but he couldn't keep up and told me to write most of them.

June came to my desk one afternoon. "We've got a problem," she said. June managed several executive branch divisions; one of those was the Correspondence Office, and usually when she came to me about a problem it was because the governor wanted some form letter rewritten. At the time, we were dealing with the first lady's announcement that she'd filed for divorce.

"We have a good many of those," I said. "Which one are you referring to?"

"The word 'integrity' is all over our letters. It's everywhere. It's not that I don't think he has integrity," she said, I thought with a smile. "It's just that when most people get a letter from him right now, they might find the word 'integrity' a little, um—."

"Ironic?"

"Off-putting. And ironic."

She handed me a folder full of form letters—a letter to newlyweds, a letter to new parents, to bereaved family members, to winners of sports awards and military medals. Each contained the word "integrity"; all had to be reworded, and usually shortened.

Condolence language had to be redone too. The governor liked to send short letters to anyone he knew or had met whose spouse or close relative had died; the composition of these letters, normally formulaic, now required thought. I could no longer use the first-person plural to refer to the governor and his wife, as in "You'll be in our thoughts and prayers." But I couldn't just change "our" to "my" since "You'll be in my thoughts and prayers" called attention to his singularity, and in any case who wants to be thought about and prayed for by a lonely disgraced politician?

Other changes were necessary. Someone in a cabinet agency noticed that a form letter signed by the governor had for years been attached to literature given to new mothers. The letter explained how the governor and his wife had always tried to view their children as precious gifts. It had to be rewritten.

Among the most severe challenges was the letter to couples newly engaged. The one I used consisted of about two hundred words, a cheery and slightly hokey paragraph about the meaning of marriage. ("More than anything, marriage is about commitment.") Instead of ceasing to send them, as both June and I told the governor would have been the wiser course, he wanted to rewrite the letter and continue the tradition, "but without saying anything weird." I had always thought that writing meaningless words must be easy, but it isn't. Try writing three uplifting sentences about marriage without in any way mentioning or alluding to marriage.

A little later, when we began once again to send out statements and press releases that had nothing to do with divorce or impeachment, I drafted a release in which it was suggested that "an honest look at the numbers" proved something or other. "It looks fine," he said after reading it. "But let's not use that word 'honest.' I'm not really in a position to lecture people about honesty." He said it with uncharacteristic sadness, and for a moment I forgave him for everything.

———

In the fall he was ready to "get back out there," to speak publicly about something other than the scandal—or, as he had begun referring to it, "that which has caused the stir that it has."

Congress was rewriting the Real ID legislation, and it was decided that the governor should hold a press conference on the administration's "concerns" about the new version. He'd do it at one of the DMV offices in the Upstate. Paul explained to me what the three concerns were, and I wrote them out in my customary way, adding a flourish or historical parallel here and there. Stewart, Nat, and I met with the governor. He was far more agitated by what the press might ask about his marriage than about anything to do with public policy.

"Look, Governor," Stewart began with his usual reassuring articulacy. There was no doubt reporters were going to hit him with a lot of questions about the divorce, the flights, Maria, and everything else. He actually said the name Maria; it felt wrong to hear anybody say it in the governor's presence. But, Stewart went on, he had to let them do it, get it out of their system. Once the governor responded in the same way a few times, they would get tired of asking.

"Okay," he said, almost appreciatively. "So let's practice."

Nat, imitating the self-consciously dignified tones reporters sometimes use, began: Would the governor be able to give the job his full attention in light of all that was happening in his personal life? "Aaaah," came the response. "I'd simply say this." His voice sounded relaxed, urbane. "I've already talked in more than enough detail about struggles on the personal front. We're trying our best to work through some issues. I'd leave it at that."

We went through a few more questions before Paul came in. There was a problem. The third of the three points the governor was to explain at the press conference—the one about Real ID not distinguishing between indictments and convictions, I think—wasn't true. We'd have to take it out. But, Paul said, we can just go with the first two; those are solid.

"So we've only got two problems with the new bill?"

"Yeah," Paul said, "but they're solid."

"Okay," the governor said, the urbanity in his voice turning immediately to aggression, "I'm not getting out there to talk about two stupid points. I need three points, first, second, third. Got that? Give me a third point. Go."

The four of us walked over to the policy office. "Okay, people," Paul said to the three or four staffers and law clerks, "we've only got two points and the boss wants three. Let's find him a third point."

Eventually they found one, but it didn't matter. Stewart's and the governor's instincts were right. There wasn't a single question about Real ID. All reporters cared about was the divorce. During the questions three college students stood behind the gaggle and ridiculed him. "Governor," one of them kept shouting, "where's your wedding ring?"

The next morning the governor walked into the press office and sat down without saying a word. Nat asked him what he thought of the press conference. The stories in the press weren't great, but they weren't terrible, and the governor had looked briefly like a governor.

"Just glad it's over," he said. "Do you know, I've never worn a wedding ring?"

———

Aaron had left for another job. Nat was now spokesman. He didn't want to do it, he told me, but the governor had a way of persuading you to do things you didn't think you'd do under any circumstances. Nat was the kind of person who would overprepare for everything, and the thought of becoming the mouthpiece of a lame duck administration in perpetual crisis seemed overwhelming to him. He'd have me practice giving him hard questions, and we both knew he didn't do particularly well. Even in ordinary conversations, he always seemed to know more than he was letting on—he had a cold, ironic sense of humor—and his answers sounded vaguely inauthentic. But he worked hard at it. Once, as we were walking to lunch, we saw Donald Hatfield, the AP reporter, a few hundred yards away. "You know," he told me, "Hatfield's worked for the AP for thirty-five years, and they've never made him bureau chief. You know why?" I said I didn't. "Because in like Nineteen-sixty-eight he killed a woman. Involuntary manslaughter. He served some time. But when he took the job with the AP, they made it a part of the deal that he couldn't be bureau chief, just because of the scandal. And he agreed."

"Are you serious?"

"No, I just made that up. How'd I do?"

———

By late fall the governor was starting to do events again. At first he had the scheduling office line up innumerable Rotary Club visits. The purported reason for these visits was the usual one, namely to go over his agenda for the upcoming legislative session. He had a modest agenda. But the real reason was to apologize to his supporters. He must have visited thirty or forty Rotaries over the following year, and at each one he would begin with a long apology. Usually it would end with some homely riff on the theme of redemption. "God's in the business of turning lemons into lemonade," he would say, occasionally reversing it: "God's in the business of making lemons out of lemonade."

Governors always have economic development announcements to attend, and he began doing these. He spoke at an announcement by a diaper company and another by a diesel engine manufacturer, and then another by a company that produced composite materials. But the strategy of doing "normal" stuff to make reporters forget about the scandal never really worked. For one thing, Donald Hatfield would show up at every event and ask the governor something about the scandal, and reporters from the national papers, the *Times*, the *Post*, *Politico*, and the others, were always showing up and asking questions about the first lady, or the former first lady as she soon became, or the mistress or the flights. But sometimes, when nothing scandal-related had happened for a few days, he could get through a whole event and no one would say anything about Maria or Argentina or divorce.

In January the legislature came back, and he delivered a modest but successful State of the State speech. It was the first and only time he ever used a teleprompter. He practiced for many hours, with me running the script, and did well on the night of the speech, although one of the teleprompter's reflectors was slightly off, and after the speech he told me angrily that he had to slouch to one side for the entire fifty minutes. You couldn't tell, though.

I don't know if I'd gotten better at my job, or if the whole affair had shaken the boss so badly that he'd forgotten how much he hated my writing, but he seemed oftener now to take what I gave him without much impatience. Occasionally, though, he couldn't be satisfied. Once, he was to speak at the grand opening of a manufacturer of electric buses. It wasn't an ideal event to write remarks for, partly because the idea of an electric bus just sounded improbable. A company of that kind survives on grant money, and that alone predisposed the governor against it; what lit his imagination was innovation springing from the profit motive, not grants and bridge loans from government entities in the name of fostering the "knowledge economy."

There was also the fact that the first lady had filed for divorce and the hearing was a few days away.

When I walked into his office to go over the event with him, he didn't look at me. "What?" he said, as if to the wall.

"The TerraPax event's tomorrow. That's the company that makes electric buses. Have you looked over the stuff I put in the speech book?"

"No. What do you have?" he replied, looking at various things on his desk but not at me. "Tell me about it."

I handed him another copy and told him about the company. He looked over what I'd written, but I had the feeling he wasn't seeing it. He just mumbled, "This is stupid . . . Stupid . . . I don't get it . . . Who cares . . . Boring." At last he looked up at me, and I could see his eyes were bloodshot. "Here's the situation," he said, "none of this is interesting. I need something that's moving, something—I don't know. I mean, what is this?" He read out a fragment or two; he was working up to a rant. "You're a bright guy. Get me something interesting. About the company, or about innovation. About buses. I don't know. I could hire any twenty-year-old to give me this stuff. This is just a poor effort." Now his eyes darted around the room. "You don't have to get up there in front of five hundred or a thousand people tomorrow. You have to have creativity for something like this, not some stupid line about"—he looked again at the paper in his hand—"the industrial revolution. These people already know about the industrial revolution. This isn't a history lecture. You can't—."

"Got it," I said.

As I walked out of the office, Stewart, who'd heard some of the exchange, murmured, "Pride cometh after the fall."

It happened once more. I gave him two pages of themes. What they were I don't remember—something about pollution at the Beijing Olympics, something about mass transit improving quality of life, and four or five other ideas. He hated them all.

I gave up. Let him figure out what to say himself, I thought.

Five or ten minutes before he was supposed to leave for the event, he burst into the office. "Okay, what am I saying at this thing? You've had time to think about it. Give me something. Go."

"Governor," I said, "I'm out. I've given you everything I can think of."

"Okay, this is pathetic." He gritted his teeth and narrowed his eyes, like a wolf. "Pathetic. I can't believe you've been with me for, what, three or four years now, and you can't think of a single interesting thing to say at a—at a—at a whatever this is. I've got to walk into this thing, not you. I've got to stand up in front of a crowd, not you. And I don't have jack to say. This is a joke."

Somehow, I don't know how, an idea came to me. It was like Nat's inspirations, only real. "What's the date?" I asked.

"Wha—?"

"The date. Isn't it the fourth?"

Nat, who was listening silently, nodded yes.

"It's Rosa Parks's birthday."

The governor just stared at me. His face softened.

"That's what you want," I said. "Rosa Parks thought about buses in a new way. What she did on a bus changed the world. What TerraPax is doing with an old idea—the bus idea—has the potential to change the world. Both take courage. The one changed society for the better and made us a better nation. The other is improving our quality of life, or the quality of our air, or something, and it has the potential to make us a better society. Something like that."

It was absolutely ridiculous, but it was perfect. I knew it and he knew it.

At last he said, "Okay. That's something. That's actually something."

———

Soon we were back to writing op-eds. But it was a trickier business now. Scores of words, phrases, and concepts were, like the governor's love story, forbidden. I couldn't use the word "family," for example, or "faith" or "cry" or "love." Any of these would have invited the ridicule of the naughtier commentators.

He was already the victim of enough double entendres without adding to the list; many a joke was made about the governor having his own "stimulus package," and "hiking on the Appalachian Trail" had become his special contribution to American slang. After I wrote the phrase "hiking taxes" it occurred to me that "hiking" would have to be changed to "raising."

Before the fall he had often alluded to his sons as members of a future generation whose income the federal government was effectively stealing by spending borrowed money. Scratch all references to the boys. Even if he'd betrayed their mother and not them, it would have sounded rich for him to affect deep concern for their well-being; the rhetorical reprisals would have been swift and painful. Before the fall he had often criticized the federal government's fiscal and monetary policies by referring to Argentina's experience with hyperinflation during the 1970s and 1980s. Obviously he couldn't say anything about Argentina, so that argument was gone. But it wasn't just Argentina. It was any South American country; they were all too close, too suggestive. Before the fall the task of writing remarks to be delivered at the opening of a Brazilian-owned manufacturing plant wouldn't have taxed my imaginative powers; now it became a challenge.

Things settled down. He wasn't invited to speak at any out-of-state events any more, but the Rotary Clubs were always happy to have him, and even a damaged governor is good enough for a ribbon-cutting ceremony, of which there seemed to be an inordinate number during that last year. The one thing that changed definitely for the worse was the sheer embarrassment of being a writer for a disgraced politician.

One minute you worked for a popular and energetic politician, one whose name was frequently mentioned (however tenuously) among those of other presidential contenders, and the next you worked for a blubbering emotional wreck of a man. Even now, when I tell people what I used to do, someone will ask, "Did you write *that* speech?" I just chuckle miserably.

The late-night shows, the columnists, the bloggers—they were relentless: always crude, often predictable and unfunny, occasionally devastating. Maria's name was part of the fun: "How do you solve a problem like Maria?" Eventually we began to enjoy the humor in it. At one point a few of us competed to produce the most apt literary quotation. The winning entry came from *The Picture of Dorian Gray*: "I have grown to love secrecy. It seems to be the one thing that can make modern life mysterious or marvelous to us. The commonest thing is delightful if one only hides it. When I leave town now I never tell my people where I am going. If I did, I would lose all my pleasure. It is a silly habit, I dare say, but somehow it brings a great deal of romance into one's life."

The governor became to us like a drunkard father. He was a monster and a lout, but he was our governor; we could ridicule him, but outsiders couldn't. So when a variety of opponents and former allies tried to capitalize on his political weakness, we responded from the soul. We disliked him severely already—some of us hated him—so if they had simply ignored him or at least been subtle in their attacks, we would have agreed with them. As it was, they tried to destroy him, and we felt obligated to fight back, hard.

The situation brings to mind Adam Ferguson, the eighteenth-century political philosopher, whose works I read at Edinburgh. Ferguson thought the spirit of rivalry, when kept within limits, had the beneficial effect of encouraging a proper affection for one's own nation or culture. Rivalry and patriotism exist, says Ferguson, in a kind of symbiotic relationship: "Our attachment to one division, or to one sect, seems often to derive much of its force from an animosity conceived to an opposite one: and this animosity in its turn, as often arises from a zeal in behalf of the side we espouse, and from a desire to vindicate the rights of our party."* Anyone who has played sports at a competitive level or worked for a underdog company fighting for market share will admit that the emotions flowing from sheer dislike of a competitor, or from an almost irrational desire to vanquish that competitor, have a way of eliciting a high level of performance.

I think of one senator especially. Even now I want to call him a pretentious semiliterate boob—which itself suggests I still have some emotional investment in defending the governor. This senator got hold of some law that state employees are required to take the least expensive option in any travel arrangements paid for by the state. It was a preposterous reason to attack the governor, or any governor, for not flying coach, but the senator was running for U.S. Congress and must have thought he could benefit from appearing to be "tough" on the adulterous governor. Well, the adulterous governor needed to

---

* *Essay on the History of Civil Society*, part 1, section 3.

be punished severely for innumerable hypocrisies—we all felt that—but we weren't going to let some bumbling opportunistic yokel abuse our old man. A good number of us got in on the effort to upend the senator. We did a little research and found that he'd taken a handful of high-dollar trips himself and that other governors had flown first class and business class—one of them had taken a transatlantic trip on the Concord—and the senator hadn't said a word about it. I don't know what, if anything, was done with that information, but the whole matter quietly fizzled and the guy's congressional campaign flopped.

It was the same when the house Judiciary Ad Hoc Committee, on which Greg Delleney sat, brought up impeachment. If Delleney had been content to limit the impeachment articles to the governor's being gone for five days without notifying proper authorities, or to lying to staff and by extension to the public about his whereabouts, either might have been a reason for considering impeachment. As it was, he had to bring up every conceivable ethical infraction: the governor had visited his mistress in Argentina while on an official visit to Brazil; he'd flown on the state plane to a supposedly political event, as if every event attended by a politician can't be construed as somehow political; and on and on. He even brought in Larry Jones II as a witness. Jones II—the prolific adulator of the governor who'd wanted him to attend some kind of philosophical gabfest—claimed he had heard the Argentine ambassador to the United States say the governor told him that he wasn't interested in expanding trade relations with Argentina, thus indicating that the Argentine leg of an economic development trip to South America must have been added for no other reason than to facilitate the governor's affair. Indeed so bitter was Jones II's disappointment in the governor that, during the administration's last year, he undertook a letter-writing campaign as fiercely critical of the governor as his former correspondence had been supplicatory.

Jakie Knotts, proud of his coup, crowed to the news media as if the governor had been caught embezzling money from a church. "How many moe shoes have gotta drop before we see the truth of this thing?" he kept asking. It all felt unjust. If they'd only stuck to the basic deed, we would have been happy to see him brought down. But not this way. And not by these people. Almost without meaning to we threw ourselves into saving the old man. Gleefully we found old flight manifests showing a good number of the governor's adversaries had used the state plane for purposes that could hardly be called official. We already knew about one senator's wanton use of his campaign account; after a little digging and asking around, we also discovered that he'd used that account for a variety of lavish indulgences that I shouldn't mention. These findings must have found their way to the offenders' mailboxes, but I never heard how.

That year's session went modestly well. A couple of bills the governor had pushed for passed the legislature; the Employment and Workforce Commission got overhauled, and one or two other things. The common explanation for this was that the governor had made himself irrelevant and therefore easier to work with: the legislature no longer cared about wrecking his presidential ambitions and so lacked a reason to oppose him on everything. But it was pretty negligible stuff compared to what we all knew the governor thought he'd be doing by this time. Signing a few modest reforms and publishing a few op-eds in state newspapers about piecemeal measures that "have the potential to make a real difference in people's lives" doesn't feel like much compared to making speeches in Iowa and meeting with billionaires about financial support and U.S. senators about endorsements. Avoiding impeachment and getting credit for restructuring the state Workforce Commission doesn't mean a lot when you have to watch in futility as the nation searches for somebody exactly like you but passes you by because you're a joke.

Still, and despite the fact that most of the media attention was now premised on his fall and not his rise, there was something about it that he couldn't help enjoying. The crowds of reporters, the incessant headlines, the necessity of responding every day to some new self-inflicted absurdity—there was something about it all that made him thrive. Once, we held a press conference about some piece of legislation or other, and in usual press conference style the governor stood behind a podium flanked by four or five grave-looking lawmakers. There were maybe two questions about the bill, whatever it was, and then Donald Hatfield asked, "Are you still seeing her—Maria?"

You could see it on the governor's face. He wanted the whole thing to go away and to become again what he had been. But not enough to ignore that question. The world was interested in his life, what he did with himself, who he was seeing, and that was a good deal better than ignoring him. He paused and looked around the room. And then he answered the question. "Well clearly, I mean, it's not going to be easy to maintain a relationship across that geographical distance, but we're working through that."

"So you are still seeing her?" Hatfield persisted.

Quietly the politicians behind the governor began slipping away.

"Wwwwwell I mean, the obvious is the obvious. In other words . . ."

Later that night I was still in the office when the governor walked in looking for Nat, who'd gone home.

"Okay," he said. He sat down.

Beyond the occasional greeting and an awkward chat at one of the mansion parties, he and I had never spoken to each other about anything unrelated to work. When you were in the car with him and the conversation inadvertently veered toward something remotely personal, he'd quickly switch topics or get on his phone or make up a reason to criticize you. Now he was sitting there for no reason, apparently needing to talk to somebody.

"What'd you think of that?" he asked.

"Well," I said. Lots of things passed through my mind, but I just sat there stupidly saying, "Well."

He waited.

At last I said, "Well, you've never been happy just saying what any politician would say. That's what got you in trouble when this whole thing blew up. Do you know Michael Jackson died the day after it all happened? The twenty-fifth. The whole thing would have been buried—maybe not buried, but almost. You couldn't stand saying the usual boring stuff, though." It felt awkward criticizing him like this, but once I'd got going I couldn't stop. "Sometimes you should just say what every other politician would say. When Hatfield asked you whether you were still seeing her, you should have just said, 'Donald, I'm not here to talk about my personal life.' But you're so addicted to being different, you just had to say something weird."

There was truth in what I told him, even if I had put it in a way that would appeal to his self-regard; I admit that. But there was truth in it. He always had to say something original, something quotable or memorable. That's why, in his notorious press conference, and in the notorious interview with the AP ("soul mate," "love story"), he'd been so incapable of simply closing his mouth. Any other politician—at least any other politician not intending to resign on the spot—would have emitted the usual rigmarole about how this was a private matter and how he was going to work through some difficult issues with his wife and how he had disappointed his family and his staff and the citizens of this great state. This governor was incapable of the usual rigmarole; his strength was his folly. Instead of giving the press formulaic balderdash, he kept rummaging through the tawdry verbiage of middle-aged love affairs trying to find something redeemable, something that would show the world that his infantile obsession with a foreign divorcée was somehow nobler or more pardonable than the sordid entanglement of an average politician.

"Yeah, I guess that's a big part of it," he said. He leaned back in the chair and stared at the ceiling. "I'm always looking for language that's—I don't know."

"Language that's what?"

He kept looking at the ceiling. "I don't mean just language, just words. It's more than words. It's conceptual. It's real. I always find myself trying to communicate something—larger."

"Larger" was one of the words on my list. He used it all the time. Sometimes he spoke of the "larger issue" or the "larger question," but usually it was the "larger notion." Sometimes he spoke of "this larger notion" of something or other in a way that made sense ("this larger notion of serving others"), but at other times it prefaced some noun phrase that couldn't be described as a "notion" at all, far less a "larger" one ("this larger notion of fairness and minimizing the tax burden on the job-creating businesses and hard-working people across this state"; "this larger notion of how well automotive companies are able to compete with counterparts elsewhere in the world"). The phrase had long been the source of jokes among staffers. "Why larger? Larger than what?" When we drafted a release or a press statement and weren't sure if he would approve it, someone would say, "Stick 'a larger notion' in there and it should be fine." I remember someone saying that if the governor ever wrote a book about God, it should be called "The Largest Notion."

"Larger?" I said.

"Yeah. I know that sounds weird. And I don't know what I mean by it exactly. It's just—I feel there's something—larger—you know, just bigger—bigger than what I'm able to communicate in words. That's what I'm after."

———

Strange things happen toward the end of an administration. One of them, in my case, was admittance to the gift room.

Politicians receive more gifts than you can imagine. Admirers send books and framed photographs and, at Christmas, specialty food items. Appreciative crowds show their gratitude to the guest speaker by presenting him with a hand-carved letter-opener or a small sculpture by a local artist. When I had traveled with the governor, I got stuck carrying the things back to the car or the plane, usually a T-shirt or a "golden" shovel (for ceremonial groundbreakings) or a giant pair of scissors (for ceremonial ribbon cuttings). Sometimes he got something genuinely interesting. At a town meeting inside the warehouse of a small metalwork company the employees presented him with a state flag they had fashioned from a sheet of copper—a three-by-five-foot rectangle with the shapes of a palmetto tree and a crescent moon cut out of it—a beautiful object in its way, and one I would have liked to have.

Ethics laws dictated that all gifts had to be recorded, along with their approximate value, and a list of them deposited with the requisite agency at the end of the year. If you were the staffer who brought the gift back to the office, you had to do this. Sometimes the governor would tell you to keep them; I got several T-shirts this way and one variety pack of floor polish. But usually you had to make up values—$10 for a T-shirt, $20 for a book, $100 for an original sculpture or a copper flag—fill out the paperwork, and give it to June for depositing in the gift room. I imagined a closet-size room somewhere in the governor's mansion crammed with decorative pillows and model cranes and framed photographs.

With a few weeks left in the term, June came into the press office and invited me and two colleagues to this room. It wasn't a closet in the governor's residence at all; it was a huge room in a dreary government building adjacent to the State House. The room was lined with tables, each covered with trinkets and gadgets and baseball caps and books. There were shot glasses, books of postcards, novelty lighters, tote bags, stacks of *Fireproof* DVDs, and innumerable coffee mugs. We were told to take anything we liked. My attention inclined to the books, but I was disappointed. There were books about counties and agricultural methods and chiropracty and the textile industry. An entire section was devoted to marriage. There were books about Baha'ism and the 1984 presidential election and a variety of foreign cities, almost all of them inscribed to the governor, but nothing I was interested in.

I did pick up a few things: a baseball cap, a beer koozie advertising some private boarding school, a white golf shirt with the BMW logo on the sleeve, a print from the National Gallery of Ireland, a tartan tie, and a ballpoint pen made of wood. I loaded them into a tote bag bearing the words Universität Stuttgart, also from the gift room. If I had to estimate the combined price of everything in that room, say for insurance purposes, I would guess $50,000. If you added the things the governor had kept for himself and his wife and sons—the great sheet-metal flag, for instance, was not in the room—as well as the hundreds of things he had regifted over the years, the combined worth must have been $100,000 or more.

A large room full of token mementos, well-meaning but

frequently inappropriate gestures, and lame attempts at ingratiation: you could interpret it as a small manifestation of modern democratic politics—full of waste, insincerity, and comic impropriety. (Did someone really think this governor would appreciate a cigarette lighter made to look like a 9mm handgun?) On the other hand, although these gifts were not extravagant—nothing I saw would have been likely to influence a policy decision—many of them had an understated quality. The tartan tie is made from clearly superior fabric, and the ballpoint pen, I later discovered, contains a laser pointer.

———

We did all the things a political office does on the way out. We sent out press statements about the need to continue reform; the boss traveled around urging tax reform; he quietly backed a candidate in the race for governor. My project was to put together an "accomplishments list," an improbably long document listing the administration's achievements in misleadingly straightforward language. ("We achieved the largest recurring tax cut in state history.") He was keenly interested in this product and badgered me relentlessly about the wording of its hundreds of items. "We've got to tell the story," he would say. "Nobody else is going to tell it for us." Which I guess was true.

With a few days left, the constant need for talking points finally ended. Those of us who hadn't left yet were interviewing for jobs elsewhere. Nat would go back to the upper Midwest to work for a large multinational corporation whose public-relations arm needed help in crisis management. Stewart found a place in the highest echelon of the state department of education. Some of my colleagues left to make large amounts of money "consulting," whatever that means. I was interviewing for a position with a small nonprofit group, and eventually took it. A few months later I would admit to myself, then more gradually to Laura, the distance I had allowed my old job to place between me and my wife.

Pictures had to come down from the office walls, desks had to be cleaned out, and the stacks of newspapers and notebooks and manila folders and old executive budgets had to be stored in boxes or thrown out. Hundreds of pages of the governor's handwritten notes for speeches, together with the note cards he used to deliver them, all had to be put in boxes and sent to the archives. It felt good to seal them up with industrial boxing tape and send them away, like burying a hateful relative.

———

The last time I saw the governor was early one weekend morning before the inauguration of his successor. I'd come in to fill out some remaining paperwork and box up a few items. When I got there, the door to his office was open. I looked in. Most of the furniture was gone. Boxes were everywhere. His office had been full of baubles given to him by admiring citizens and sundry companies and organizations: a toy crane, a replica passenger jet, a small palmetto tree made exclusively of bottle caps. Until a few days before, there had been framed pictures everywhere: pictures of the governor with his family, of the governor with other famous politicians, of the governor with various hardhat-wearing dignitaries holding shovels at groundbreaking ceremonies. Now the walls were bare, the pictures packed away. His desk was gone. A great stack of books he'd been intending to read was gone too.

The governor was there, alone as far as I could tell. He sat on one of the remaining chairs looking at a few of the pictures that hadn't yet been stored away. He held one in his hands and gazed at it silently. I couldn't make it out and wondered if it was a picture of his sons or his wife. He looked at it for a long time. When he put it down, he just sat silently.

Was he at last pondering the ruin he'd created? Maybe in part, but I doubt he thought of it as ruin. The word suggests finality, and I was sure that this man would not accept any form of finality until his heart stopped beating. He had been ready to pick up the pieces almost as soon as he'd strewn them on the ground; resigning may have been an option for a few days, but leaving the public sphere never was. I was sure of it. When people asked me what he planned to do after leaving office, I would say I didn't know but expected he would start figuring out what office to run for next. That would get a laugh, but I meant it, and I knew I was right. Men like him think of achievement and victory, not of failure, and when they fail disastrously their first thought is not to repair the damage but to gauge how far it is to the next victory. Of course this isn't a new insight. Politicians have dishonored themselves and embarrassed their families and allies many times before, and their staff—sometimes in books like this one—have expressed shock and dismay at the way their chiefs have wanted to make it all go away with a few insincere apologies. Why do we continue to trust these men?

Let me ask that question in a more pointed way: Why do we trust men who have sought and attained high office by innumerable acts of vanity and self-will? When a work colleague makes a habit of insisting on his own competence and virtue, we may tolerate him, we may even admire his work, but his vanity is not an inducement to trust him. Why, then, do we trust the men who make careers of persuading us of their goodness and greatness, and who compete for our votes? Catherine Zuckert makes this point powerfully in an essay on *Tom Sawyer*. Tom, remember, is brave and clever and has a firm sense of the right thing to do, but he is animated mainly by a hunger for glory. He is, in short, the essence of an able politician. "People like Tom Sawyer serve others not for the sake of the others," writes Zuckert. "They serve because they glory in receiving glory. . . . We should reward such people with the fame they so desire—if and when they perform real public services. But we should not trust them."[†] I feel the force of that last sentence now: we go badly wrong when we trust them. Indeed much of the hand-wringing commentary about the loss of trust in government resulting from Vietnam and Watergate is simply, I now think, a failure to appreciate the simple truth that politicians should never have been

---

† Catherine Zuckert, "Tom Sawyer: Potential President," in *Democracy's Literature*, edited by Patrick Deneen and Joseph Romance (Lanham, MD: Roman and Littlefield, 2005), 61–78 (76).

trusted in the first place. They may be lauded when they're right and venerated when they're dead, but they should never be trusted.

I say all this confidently now, but it wasn't that long ago that I thought the answer to all our social and political problems was to elect the right people—good people with the right ideas and the courage to act on them. Before I went to work for the governor, I thought he was one of the right people. And he was. He did what he said he was going to do, he took his duties seriously, he behaved himself in public with charm and decorum, he did not fear criticism, and he had realistic views of what government could and couldn't accomplish. He was everything a politician should be—a politician in the best sense of that word, if it has a best sense. After two or three weeks of working for him, though, I knew something was wrong. It wasn't that I thought he should have been the same thoughtful political leader in private that he was in public; the difference between public persona and reality is a valuable and inevitable one. Rather, I found it unnerving to discover such a stark difference between the personality he presented to the public and the one to which he subjected his staff. I remarked on this difference many times to my wife during that first year. We often laughed about it, but I think we both knew it signified something terrible—not just about the governor but about the world, or at least about democratic cultures in which political leaders often function as celebrities and even heroes. What that something was came to me much later, when I glimpsed the depth of his self-absorption. Here was a man who shattered his ambitions and humiliated his family and friends by pursuing his own petty, myopic desires. And yet in his ruin he could not find more than the paltriest shred of genuine self-criticism. I believe he wanted to feel a deeper remorse, but he looked inside and it wasn't there. All he found was more of himself.

And if that was true of him, it wasn't true only of him. It was true to one degree or another of all politicians. So the axiom on which I had unconsciously based my thinking for years—that what we needed was to elect the right people, good people, smart and wise and principled people—had been a delusion. That's probably putting it too strongly. We should want to elect wise and principled people, but once you think of them as wise and principled, you trust them, and at about the time you trust them, they undermine your trust and you've got to find someone else. So I realized that the men in whom I had placed my hopes could at any moment fall victim to vain impulses and self-addiction and so make clowns of themselves and ruin the causes for which they claimed to fight.

I must sound hopelessly naïve. Hadn't I noticed that politicians are prone to vanity, and that vanity frequently unmakes them? Yes, I had noticed. But I had thought of it mainly as a joke. Now I realized it wasn't a joke. It was the most important thing.

Self-regard isn't a foible to which some politicians are vulnerable. It is the peculiar and deadly flaw of modern democratic politics. Let me explain what I mean, briefly. There have been essentially three ways of arranging a constitutionally limited government, three ways of placing men under the authority of other men according to preordained laws. The first is by submitting to a constitutionally limited monarch. Subjects love or at least respect the king because of who he is: he is theirs, just as his father was before him. If the king is a fool or a tyrant, he is still the king and entitled to reverence, though not to obedience in every respect; only if he breaks the bond between himself and his subjects entirely can he be thrown out. The second is by establishing some form of meritocracy. No political entity can achieve complete meritocracy because merit, although we know it when we see it, or at least we think we do, is too hard to define and impossible to predict. Greater or lesser forms of meritocracy existed (in the English-speaking world) from the time of Oliver Cromwell to the mid-twentieth century. It was Cromwell who rejected the practice of appointing aristocratic and royal favorites and pursued the principle that men should be chosen according to their capabilities rather than their blood ties and social connections. During this era meritocracy mixed with both democracy and aristocracy, sometimes tending in one direction, sometimes in the other, but the essential idea was government by people qualified to govern. That ideal was still at least theoretically practicable in Western democracies until the principle of universal suffrage began its ascendency. At our nation's founding, remember, the idea that everybody should have the right to vote was the crazy dream of a few radicals; in most places only property owners could vote, state legislatures elected U.S. senators, and electors chosen by legislators elected presidents. What's left to us now is the third form of constitutional government: giving authority to men and women chosen by simple majorities. Since we don't believe in hereditary royal authority, and since we've accepted the idea that virtually everyone should have the vote, we have no choice but to confer power on those who can persuade most of us that they'll use it well. Successful politicians are people who know how to make us think well of them without our realizing that that's what they're doing; they know how to make us admire and trust them.

I don't say any of this to demean politicians. It takes an able and industrious person to do what they do, and many of them are capable of courage and honorable conduct. But the same can be said of traveling salesmen; it does not follow that we should trust them. The brutal reality is that politicians gain power by convincing us that they are wise and trustworthy. What they do isn't in fact very different from the classical arts of rhetoric or oratory. Most modern politicians, and certainly the one I worked for, are not orators in the common sense of the word, but they use language, timing, and images to win electoral and legislative victories, just as the Sophists did in the fourth and fifth centuries BC. In Plato's *Gorgias*, Socrates reviles rhetoric as a form of "flattery," sometimes translated as "pandering": "the ghost or counterfeit of a branch of politics." Flattery "pretends to be that which it simulates," says Socrates, "and having no regard for men's highest interests, is ever making pleasure the bait of the unwary, and deceiving them into the belief that it is of the highest value to them." Rhetoricians, in other words—politicians—please the masses not by actually doing wise and virtuous things with state power but by making the masses believe that that's what they are doing, or that that's what they want to do, or that that's what they would do if more power were given to them. We could press Socrates on whether he really believes it's all a matter of pleasure, but there is an undeniable kind of pleasure to be had in a politician's expression of a message we approve of, or of any powerful person's enunciation of our own views. When the governor speculated that the administration in Washington was attempting to create a "savior-based economy," the effect had an almost aesthetic quality to it, like reading a line of poetry that encapsulates a thought you didn't even know you had until you read it.

The problem was that the governor wanted to be a savior himself. His ideas were sound, his views genuinely held, and at crucial times he showed great courage in holding to them—the kind of defiant fearlessness we long for in politics. But he was a politician, and so he had a direct personal interest in others believing these things about him. Acclaim and attention were his highest aim—just as they are every determined politician's highest aim: the praise, the fawning, the seriousness with which people take their remarks, the gaze of audiences, the way a crowded room falls silent when they enter. When we revere a politician and give him our vote, we do so because we believe his most fervent desire is to contribute to the nation's well-being or to make the right decisions with public money. That may be *a* desire, but it is not what drives him. What drives him is the thirst for glory; the public good, as he understands it, is a means to that end. So when a great statesman accomplishes a laudable goal by sagacity and bravery, we're right to give him the praise he craves. But when we're surprised and disgusted because the man we lauded has humiliated himself and disgraced his office, we haven't just misjudged a man—we've misjudged the nature of modern politics.

In the office, amid the empty walls and taped-up boxes, I stood there watching the governor for another minute or two. He didn't move for a long time but sat staring at a shuttered window. Perhaps he was thinking of what he would do next or whether greater things lay ahead.

I backed quietly out of the room and went home.

ABOUT THE AUTHOR

Barton Swaim, a South Carolinian since age three, attended the University of South Carolina and the University of Edinburgh. From 2007 to 2010 he worked for Mark Sanford, the state's governor, as a communications officer and speechwriter. He lives in Columbia with his wife, Laura, and three daughters, and writes regularly for the *Wall Street Journal* and the *Times Literary Supplement*.

4/16 - 10 + 2